ACKNOWLEDGMENTS

A special thanks to all those who have contributed to my knowledge and brought the book together. Mum & Dad, for teaching and encouraging me to appreciate boutique and craft alcohol instead of abuse.
Sam & Josh, who taught me so much of my foundation knowledge in the mixology and alcohol world. Cliff & Tom, for the hours of work put into photographing and editing hundreds of photos.
Fleur, for designing and creating the book and brand.
Madison, for writing and editing the text. And of course, to Mike, for encouraging me to create the book and bringing it all alive!

Authors: George Grbich and Madison Fisher
Design: Fleur Curac
Website: nzginguide.com
Instagram: @nzginguide
Facebook: Guide to New Zealand Gin

PUBLISHED BY
People Media Group
Newmarket, Auckland
peoplemediagroup.co.nz

CONTENTS

4   **STYLES OF GIN**

5   **THE TEAM**

6   **CLASSIC GIN**

8   batch10 New Zealand Gin

10   Black Collar Gin

12   Black Robin Rare Gin

14   Broken Heart Gin

16   Angel's Share Gin

18   Championz Gin

20   Curiosity Gin – Curious Dry

22   Dancing Sands Dry Gin

24   Denzien Te Aro Dry Gin

26   Denzien Our Coast Gin

28   Day Off Gin

30   Reikorangi Triple Distilled Dry Gin

32   Juno Extra Fine

34   Lighthouse Gin Original

36   Little Biddy Gin – Classic

38   Verdigris New Zealand Dry Gin

40   Reid + Reid Native Gin

42   Reid + Reid Rev. Dawson's Gin

44   Roots Marlborough Dry Gin

46   Scapegrace Classic

48   Solace Dry Gin

50   The Source Gin

52   Victor Gin Original

54   Waitoki Gin

56   Wild Diamond Rare Dry Gin

58   1919 Classic Gin

60   **CONTEMPORARY GIN**

62   Ariki Ultra Premium Gin

64   The Bureaucrat

66   The Doyenne

68   The Bond Store Kawakawa Gin

70   Curiosity Gin – Recipe #23

72   Denzien Smoke & Embers Gin

74   Dr Beak New Zealand Premium Gin

76   The Artist

78   The Novelist

80   The Poet

82   The Vintner

84   Grey Lynn Gin

86   East Block 200

88   Albertine

90   Original Island Gin

92   Black Label Tangelo Blossom Island Gin

94   Juno Summer 2020 Seasonal Gin

96   Juno Autumn 2020 Seasonal Gin

98   Juno Winter 2020 Seasonal Gin

100 Juno Spring 2020 Seasonal Gin

102 Little Biddy Gin – Gold Label

104 Little Biddy Gin – Black Label

106 Adorn Beauty Gin

108 Hemp Gin

110 New Zealand Native Gin – The Proof

112 1743 Riot

114 1920 Rose

116 Scapegrace Black

118 Totara Gin

120 Victor Gin Kaffir Lime

122 PINK & FLAVOURED GIN

124 batch10 Pink Gin

126 Blush Boysenberry Gin

128 Blush Rhubarb Gin

130 Blush Summer Citrus Gin

132 Broken Heart Pinot Noir Gin

134 Broken Heart Quince Gin

136 Broken Heart Rhubarb Gin

138 Black Dorris Plum

140 Curisoity Gin – Pinot Barrel Sloe

142 Curiosity Gin – Ruby

144 Dancing Sands Chocolate Gin

146 Dancing Sands Saffron Gin

148 Dancing Sands Sun-Kissed Gin

150 Day Off Feijoa Gin

152 Damson Plum & Blackberry Gin Liqueur

154 Reikorangi Rhubarb and Raspberry Gin

156 Lavender Infused Gin

158 Saffron Infused Gin

160 Little Biddy Gin – Pink

162 Adorn Rosé Beauty Gin

164 Solace Cranberry & Raspberry Gin

166 Sheep Milk & Honey Gin

168 Wild Diamond Feijoa Gin

170 Wild Diamond Vanilla Gin

172 Wild Diamond Saffron Gin

174 1919 Pineapple Bits Gin

176 1919 Pink Gin

178 BARREL AGED GIN

180 Broken Heart Barrel Aged Gin

182 Curiosity Gin – Negroni Special

184 Dancing Sands Barrel Aged Gin

186 The Pioneer

188 Black Barn Syrah Barrel Aged Gin

190 Little Biddy Gin – Cask Aged (Pinot Noir)

192 Reid + Reid Barrel Aged Gin

194 NAVY STRENGTH GIN

196 Broken Heart Navy Strength Gin

198 Dancing Sands Wasabi Strength Gin

200 Navy Strength Island Gin

202 Lighthouse Gin Hawthorn Edition

204 Scapegrace Gold

206 FEVER-TREE

207 A Short History on Tonic

208 How to Create the Perfect Gin & Tonic

210 Tonics

211 Gingers

212 Sodas

STYLES OF GIN

Dry Gin – Gins that have a predominant juniper flavour, all flavours must be added pre-distillation using natural botanicals.

Distilled Gin – Distilled the same way as dry gin, although you may add natural botanicals or artificial flavours post-distillation before bottling.

Contemporary Gin – Gins that have a predominant flavour of anything other than juniper. Juniper is always present, but the overall character will emphasize the other botanicals over the juniper.

Pink Gin – A classic style gin traditionally flavoured with Angostura Bitters, the modern versions usually use botanicals such as Strawberry, Raspberry or Red Currant to give them their unique pink colour.

Flavoured Gins – Distilled gins with one or more specifically noted and predominant botanicals other than juniper.

Barrel Aged – Gins that have been aged post-distillation in any wooden barrel for a chosen length of time.

Navy Strength – Gins bottled at an alcohol strength of at least 57% ABV.

Gin Liqueur – Distilled gins that have been infused with additional flavourings and sweetened. The alcohol content will be lower, usually between 20-30% ABV.

WE HAVE CONDENSED THE 95 NZ GINS INTO 5 CATEGORIES'

Classic – containing dry and distilled gins

Contemporary – containing contemporary gins

Pink & Flavoured – containing pink, flavoured and gin liqueurs

Barrel Aged – containing barrel aged gins

Navy Strength – containing navy strength gins

Our tasters have selected a top pick in each category. Look out for this badge.

THE TEAM

GEORGE GRBICH
Managing Editor

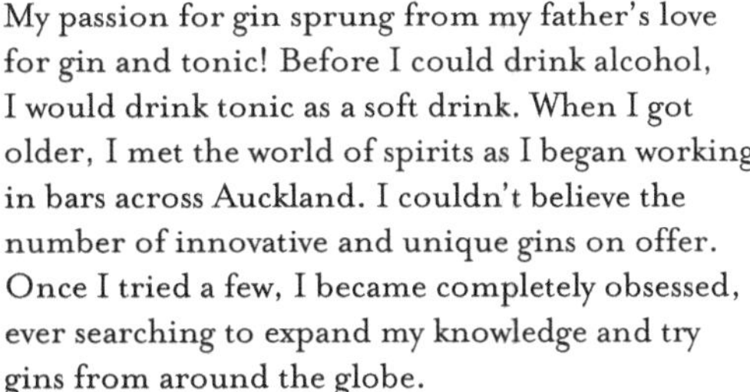

My passion for gin sprung from my father's love for gin and tonic! Before I could drink alcohol, I would drink tonic as a soft drink. When I got older, I met the world of spirits as I began working in bars across Auckland. I couldn't believe the number of innovative and unique gins on offer. Once I tried a few, I became completely obsessed, ever searching to expand my knowledge and try gins from around the globe.

After persistently trying to convince my wine drinking boss, Mike, to switch over to gin, he finally gave in to me and started to explore the gin world. One day Mike stumbled across a Gin Guide in a book store, he decided we should take my passion further, proposing the task of writing a book on New Zealand's ever growing gin industry.

STEVE BENNETT
Taster

Steve Bennett, Master of Wine, has more than 30 years of experience working in the retail, importation, distribution, production, and educational sectors of the liquor industry. In 1994 he became the youngest ever of only 450 people to have passed the Master of Wine Examination since its inception in 1953. Steve has educated both consumers and liquor industry professionals in NZ, Australia, the US, UK, and Europe.

As well as a strong professional interest in wine, Steve has a personal passion for beer and gin which he has tasted widely during his international travels.

SCOTT O'CONNOR
Taster

Scott O'Connor has spent 12 years working in hospitality throughout the UK, Spain, Australia, and New Zealand. Leaving the UK in 2019, to become general manager of The Churchill, New Zealand's highest rooftop bar, which specialises in gin with nearly 200 from around the globe. Scott's extensive beverage knowledge runs deep with over a decades experience producing countless beverage lists and signature cocktail menus.

CLASSIC

CONTAINING DRY AND DISTILLED GINS

Dry Gin – Gins that have a predominant juniper flavour, all flavours must be added pre-distillation using natural botanicals.

Distilled Gin – Distilled the same way as dry gin, although you may add natural botanicals or artificial flavours post-distillation before bottling.

———————

batch10 New Zealand Gin

37% ABV

DISTILLERY: batch10 Spirits, Puhoi
WEBSITE: batch10.com

BOTANICALS: Juniper, Coriander Seed, Cassia Bark, Angelica Root, Nutmeg, Citrus Peel, Tangerine, Orris Root, Star Anise, Anise, Lemon, Orange & Cardamom

---

TASTING NOTES: Aromatic juniper with a hint of nutmeg and star anise developing on the nose. Dry palate with a subtle spiced earth complexity leading into the finish with a lift of lemon peel.

SERVING SUGGESTION: Enjoy with Fever-Tree Premium Indian Tonic Water and a slice of lemon.

Located in the idyllic backwoods of Puhoi, batch10 Spirits was started by a bunch of mates in one of their sheds infusing premium bourbon with local native bush honey. Having grown and developed since then they now make a range of distilled spirits crafted from the finest New Zealand and international ingredients.

A classic style gin with a New Zealand twist, batch10 New Zealand Gin is smooth and crisp with a distinct hint of citrus that honours the orchards of the nearby Omaha and Matakana areas.

batch10
New Zealand
GIN

Black Collar Gin

42% ABV

DISTILLERY: Black Collar Distillery, Kerikeri

WEBSITE: blackcollardistillery.com

BOTANICALS: Juniper, Coriander Seed, Liquorice Root, Marshmallow & Others Not Disclosed

---

TASTING NOTES: Aromatic sweet lemon and lifted juniper on the nose. Bright citrus palate with a burst of floral spice and a hint of sweet liquorice with a long dry finish.

SERVING SUGGESTION: Enjoy with Fever-Tree Mediterranean Tonic Water and a slice of grapefruit.

AWARDS: IWSC UK – Bronze Medal 2019

Situated near Kerikeri in the tranquil Bay of Islands, the beating heart of Black Collar is their gorgeous handmade copper pot still called 'Frankie'. Completely old school with no automation or computer programs, it's all down to the knowledge and fine tuning of the distiller to capture just the right qualities to produce their gin.

A classic style gin, Black Collar Gin is made traditionally by macerating their botanicals overnight before distillation with no vapour infusion, water baths, essences or artificial flavourings.

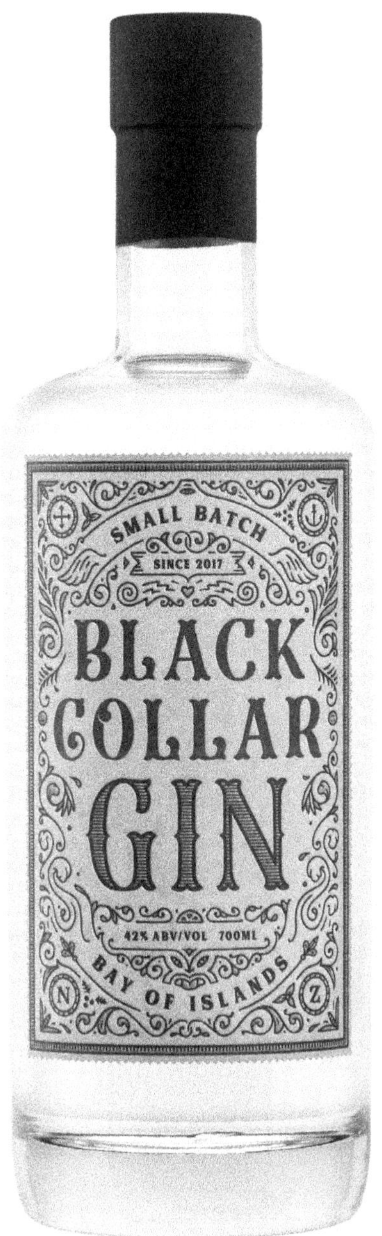

SMALL BATCH
SINCE 2017
BLACK
COLLAR
GIN
42% ABV/VOL 700ML
BAY OF ISLANDS

Black Robin Rare Gin

43% ABV

DISTILLERY: Distillerie Deinlein, Te Puna
WEBSITE: blackrobingin.co.nz

BOTANICALS: Juniper, Chervil, Watercress, Parsley, Mint, Liquorice Root, Star Anise, Horopito, Candied Lime Zest, Candied Lemon Zest & Lemongrass

---

TASTING NOTES: Light earthy juniper with peppery horopito on the nose. A clean palate with juniper richness and a hint of liquorice sweetness with a long dry finish.

SERVING SUGGESTION: Enjoy with Fever-Tree Mediterranean Tonic Water and a slice of lime.

AWARDS: San Francisco World Spirits Competition – Silver Medal 2014 & 15, 'The Fifty Best' Best Gin Awards – Double Gold 2016, Sip Awards – Gold 2015 & Consumers Choice Award 2015, and London Spirits Competition – Silver 2020

Sequestered away between the Kaimai Ranges and Tauranga, Black Robin uses a copper reflux still operated by a master distiller that can trace their distilling heritage back 90 years to Germany. Inspired by and named for the very rare and endangered Chatham Island's Black Robin, they donate to Forest & Bird for every bottle sold to help protect NZ's native wildlife and wild places for future generations.

A classic style gin, Black Robin Rare Gin is five times distilled with a unique blend of botanicals, including some native to New Zealand to honour the Black Robin's heritage. The bottle's Black Robin artwork was originally hand-painted by renowned NZ artist Andrew Barns-Graham.

CHATHAM ISLANDS
BLACK
ROBIN
RARE GIN
Distilled &
Bottled In
NEW ZEALAND
BR
43% Alc/Vol | 750ml
NEW ZEALAND
ENDANGERED

Broken Heart Gin

40% ABV

DISTILLERY: Broken Heart Spirits, Arrow Junction
VISIT THEM: 3 Whitechapel Road, Arrow Junction (by appointment)
WEBSITE: brokenheartspirits.com

BOTANICALS: Juniper, Coriander Seed, Lavender, Angelica Root
& Others Not Disclosed

TASTING NOTES: Lifted juniper with fresh aromatic lemon and lime on the
nose. A dry, clean palate with earthy spice and floral lavender developing.
Lingering floral juniper on the finish.

SERVING SUGGESTION: Enjoy with Fever-Tree Mediterranean Tonic Water
and a slice of orange.

AWARDS: NZ Spirit Awards – Double Gold 2020,
and IWSC – Silver 2016, 2017 & 2020

Nestled in the foothills of the Southern Alps near picturesque Arrowtown,
Broken Heart Spirits was born from the memory of a beloved life lost. They
endeavour to create gin that captures the glory days of a friendship between
two Germans that met in the South Island and bonded over their mutual
appreciation for creating fine spirits before one of them tragically passed away.

A classic style gin, Broken Heart Gin balances earthy, floral, spicy, and
fresh flavour profiles to capture the essence of a dry Central Otago summer.

BROKEN HEART
GIN
Distilled in the Pure South of New Zealand
BROKEN HEART
GIN
Distilled in the Pure South of New Zealand
40% ALC BY VOL.   700ML | NZ MADE

Angel's Share Gin

40% ABV

DISTILLERY: Broken Heart Spirits, Arrow Junction
VISIT THEM: 3 Whitechapel Road, Arrow Junction (by appointment)
WEBSITE: brokenheartspirits.com

BOTANICALS: Juniper, Coriander Seed, Lavender, Angelica Root
& Others Not Disclosed

TASTING NOTES: Bold aromatic juniper with a lemon, rosemary, and pine complexity on the nose. A clean, dry palate with bold juniper followed by a burst of earthy spice and subtle citrus. Long lingering juniper and a subtle hint of lavender on the finish.

SERVING SUGGESTION: Enjoy with Fever-Tree Mediterranean Tonic Water and a sprig of rosemary.

AWARDS: NZ Spirit Awards — Gold 2020

Nestled in the foothills of the Southern Alps near picturesque Arrowtown, Broken Heart Spirits was born from the memory of a beloved life lost. They endeavour to create gin that captures the glory days of a friendship between two Germans that met in the South Island and bonded over their mutual appreciation for creating fine spirits before one of them tragically passed away.

A classic style gin, Broken Heart Angel's Share Gin is a collector's edition made in small batches that play on the frontiers of balance with its botanicals.

ROKEN HEART
ANGELS
SHARE
BROKEN HEART
Collector's Edition
BATCH No
01
BOTTLE No
001 | 500
Small Batch
Distilled
Joerg Henkenhof
DISTILLER
500 ML
ANGEL'S GIN SHARE
40% ALC/VOL

Championz Gin

40% ABV

DISTILLERY: Kiwi Spirits Distillery, Motupipi
VISIT THEM: 430 Abel Tasman Drive, Motupipi
WEBSITE: kiwispiritdistillery.co.nz

BOTANICALS: Not Disclosed

TASTING NOTES: Fresh aromatic lemongrass and zesty citrus on the nose. A clean and very dry palate with heavy juniper and lemon, fresh gentle finish with subtle notes of cinnamon and cardamom.

SERVING SUGGESTION: Enjoy with Fever-Tree Aromatic Tonic Water and a slice of lemon.

AWARDS: China Wine and Spirit Awards — Double Gold 2020, New York World Spirit Awards -Silver 2019, and New Zealand Spirit Awards - Bronze 2020

Sheltered in the beautiful Golden Bay area of the Tasman region, Championz are a world away from the hustle and bustle of city life. Focusing on small batch distillation to deliver superior quality, they are committed to attention to detail and using all-natural ingredients to produce the best preservative-free spirits. They endeavour to minimise their impact on the world by taking a sustainable approach to their craft.

A classic style gin, Championz Gin is a dry gin made with water from the nearby Te Waikoropupū Springs, often considered the clearest spring water in the world.

DISTILLED IN NEW ZEALAND
A GIN FOR SPORTS LOVERS
Premium
SMALL BATCH RELEASE
CHAMPION GIN
EXHIBITS ATTRIBUTES OF A TRUE CHAMPION
LIMITED EDITION
40% ALC/VOL
80 PROOF
750ml

Curiosity Gin - Curious Dry

40% ABV

DISTILLERY: The Spirits Workshop Distillery, Christchurch
VISIT THEM: 11 Sandyford Street, Sydenham, Christchurch
WEBSITE: thespiritsworkshop.co.nz

BOTANICALS: Juniper, Tarata, Kawakawa, Horopito & Manuka

TASTING NOTES: Light juniper with horopito and kawakawa aromas.
Dry juniper palate with tarata emerging and subtle floral sweetness
on the finish.

SERVING SUGGESTION: Enjoy with Fever-Tree Mediterranean Tonic Water
and a slice of lemon.

AWARDS: Monde Awards – Gold 2017, San Francisco World Spirits
Competition – Bronze 2018, SIP Awards – Silver 2018,
and NZ Spirits Awards – Bronze 2020

Established in the light industrial area of Christchurch's suburb Sydenham,
Curiosity Gin set out from the start to create truly unique and individual
gins that stand out from the crowd. To hold true to these values their gins
are made "grain to glass" where possible, in small batches using their copper
pot still.

A classic style gin, Curiosity Gin – Curious Dry is designed for the
traditional gin drinker, made with the finest imported juniper and just four
other botanicals all of which are native to New Zealand.

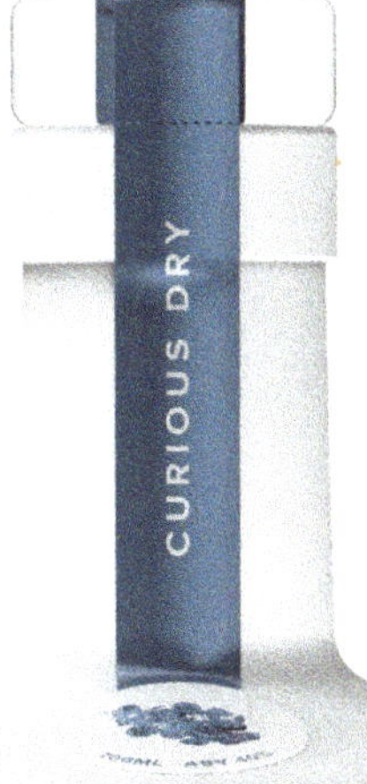

CURIOUS DRY
CURIOSITY GIN
CURIOSITY GIN

Dancing Sands Dry Gin
44% ABV

DISTILLERY: Dancing Sands Distillery, Takaka
VISIT THEM: 46A Commercial Street, Takaka
WEBSITE: dancingsands.com

BOTANICALS: Juniper, Coriander Seed, Angelica Root, Manuka, Cardamom, Peppercorn, Almond & Liquorice Root

---

TASTING NOTES: Bold pine and earthy spice aromas on the nose. Dry palate with zesty citrus, cardamom spice, and lemon freshness through to the finish.

SERVING SUGGESTION: Enjoy with Fever-Tree Premium Indian Tonic Water and a slice of lemon.

AWARDS: San Francisco World Spirit Awards – Gold Medal 2017, Silver Medal 2018 & 19, The Gin Masters – Gold 2017 & 18, and NZ Spirits Awards – Silver 2019

Bundled away in the small town of Takaka in the Tasman region's beautiful Golden Bay area, Dancing Sands Distillery sources their water from the aquifer that feeds the nearby Te Waikoropupū Springs, often regarded as the clearest spring water in the world. They make all of their gins in small 150 litre batches to allow for maximum control over quality without any automation, instead using taste, temperature, and touch to achieve their results.

A classic style gin, Dancing Sands Dry Gin is double distilled and vapour infused with eight botanicals including green manuka leaves.

DANCING SANDS
••• DRY GIN •••
44% ABV
700ML
HANDCRAFTED & MADE IN
NEW ZEALAND

Denzien Te Aro Dry Gin

42% ABV

DISTILLERY: Denzien Urban Distillery, Wellington
VISIT THEM: 10 Lombard Street, Te Aro, Wellington
WEBSITE: denzien-urban-distillery.business.site

BOTANICALS: Juniper, Horopito, Kawakawa, Lemon Peel, Orange Peel, Coriander Seed, Fennel Seed, Angelica Root, Liquorice Root & Orris Root

---

TASTING NOTES: Aromatic juniper with zesty lemon, horopito and earthy kawakawa on the nose. A clean, dry palate with bold juniper notes. Subtle tones of earthy root and fennel on the finish.

SERVING SUGGESTION: Enjoy with Fever-Tree Premium Indian Tonic Water and a slice of lemon.

AWARDS: NZ Spirits Awards – Trophy Winner Best New Zealand Product in Category & Best Overall in Category 2019, Gold 2019, Silver 2020

Standing in the heart of Wellington's vibrant central Te Aro suburb, Denzien Urban Distillery is an artisan gin distillery with a mission to make brazen city gins for city people. They produce small batches in their handmade copper pot still and use distilled rainwater, all of which can be watched in person before tasting at their visitable location.

A classic style gin, Denzien Te Aro Dry Gin is based on a London Dry Gin with a Kiwi twist.

HAND CRAFTED IN WELLINGTON
DENZIEN™
URBAN DISTILLERY
SMALL GIN BATCH
OF NEW ZEALAND
700ml
42%ABV
TE ARO DRY
UNASHAMEDLY URBAN GIN

Denzien Our Coast Gin

42% ABV

DISTILLERY: Denzien Urban Distillery, Wellington
VISIT THEM: 10 Lombard Street, Te Aro, Wellington
WEBSITE: denzien-urban-distillery.business.site

BOTANICALS: Juniper, Marlborough Sea Salt, Kelp, Black Cardamom, White Peppercorns, Wormwood, Coriander Seed, Angelica Root, Fennel Seed, Liquorice Root & Orris Root

---

TASTING NOTES: Aromatic juniper with peppery notes and vanilla sweetness on the nose. Dry, bold spice led palate with notes of peppercorn, cardamom and fennel carried by the juniper and finished with a subtle lemon and herbal freshness.

SERVING SUGGESTION: Enjoy with Fever-Tree Mediterranean Tonic Water and a slice of lemon.

AWARDS: NZ Spirits Awards — Silver 2020

Standing in the heart of Wellington's vibrant central Te Aro suburb, Denzien Urban Distillery is an artisan gin distillery with a mission to make brazen city gins for city people. They produce small batches in their handmade copper pot still and use distilled rainwater, all of which can be watched in person before tasting at their visitable location.

A classic style gin, Denzien Our Coast Gin calls upon New Zealand's coastal and island identities by using native kelp and Marlborough sea salt as botanicals.

HAND CRAFTED IN WELLINGTON
DENZIEN
URBAN DISTILLERY
SMALL GIN BATCH
OF NEW ZEALAND
700ml
42%ABV
OUR COAST
UNASHAMEDLY URBAN GIN

Day Off Gin

45% ABV

DISTILLERY: Good George Distillery, Hamilton
WEBSITE: goodgeorge.co.nz

BOTANICALS: Juniper, Coriander Seed, Angelica Root, Rosehip, Liquorice Root, Pink Peppercorns, Mandarin, Star Anise & Cardamon

---

TASTING NOTES: Lifted juniper with dried fruit and floral citrus on the nose. Clean, dry palate delivering lemon freshness and earth spiced juniper, finishing with a subtle suggestion of confected Turkish Delight.

SERVING SUGGESTION: Enjoy with Fever-Tree Mediterranean Tonic Water and a slice of lemon.

AWARDS: NZ Spirits Awards – Silver 2020 and London Spirits Competition – Bronze 2020

Cloistered in the industrial suburb of Frankton in Hamilton, Good George Distillery resides in the former St George's Church from which they take their name. Originally started as a brewery, they also began making hand sanitiser in early 2020 as part of Operation Helping Hands and later decided to give their stills a day off from that project and make some gin too.

A classic style gin, Good George: Day Off Gin is designed to evoke the concept behind its namesake and be enjoyed while relaxing.

BOTTLE NO. 001
SMALL BATCH DISTILLED IN
GOOD George DISTILLING
THE OLD SAINT GEORGE CHURCH
16
17
DAY OFF
HAND CRAFTED
750 ML
GIN
45% ABV
SMALL BATCH NEW ZEALAND DISTILLED

Reikorangi Triple Distilled Dry Gin

42% ABV

DISTILLERY: imagination, Reikorangi

WEBSITE: imaginationgin.nz

BOTANICALS: Juniper, Coriander Seed, Cinnamon, Liquorice Root, Orris Root, Orange, Lime, Lemon & Manuka

---

TASTING NOTES: Bold aromatic juniper with cinnamon and fragrant orange on the nose. A clean, rich juniper palate with apple tart-like cinnamon spice and emerging citrus on the finish.

SERVING SUGGESTION: Enjoy with Fever-Tree Refreshingly Light Indian Tonic Water and a slice of orange.

AWARDS: NZ Spirits Awards – Gold 2020, SIP Awards – Gold 2019 & 20, IWSC World Awards – Bronze 2019, and London Spirit Awards – Silver 2020

Sheltered in the lush foothills of the Reikorangi Valley on the Kapiti Coast, imagination is housed on the original site of the pioneering Tuatara Beer Brewery which they use to draw inspiration from. They produce small batch seasonal gins using a copper plate fractionating column still and pure rainwater captured on the property, and source many of their ingredients locally from family owned operations and backyard gardeners.

A classic style gin, Reikorangi Triple Distilled Dry Gin aims to create a rustic craft edge with the use of whole oranges, lemons, and limes among its other botanicals.

imagination is the only weapo
imagination
REIKORANGI
TRIPLE DISTILLED
NEW ZEALAND
DRY GIN
ABV 42% | 700ml

Juno Extra Fine

40% ABV

DISTILLERY: Begin Distilling, New Plymouth
VISIT THEM: 16 Sunley Street, Westown, New Plymouth
WEBSITE: junogin.com

BOTANICALS: Juniper, Coriander Seed, Angelica Root, Orris Root, Kaffir Lime Leaf, Manuka, Orange, Black Peppercorns, Cardamom & Cassia

---

TASTING NOTES: Aromatic juniper with kaffir lime and zesty orange freshness on the nose. A clean, dry palate bursting with kaffir lime. Distinctive peppery spice emerging on the finish.

SERVING SUGGESTION: Enjoy with Fever-Tree Mediterranean Tonic Water and a slice of lime.

AWARDS: San Francisco World Spirits Competition – Silver 2018 & Double Gold Packaging Design Award 2018, IWSC London – Silver 2019, Singapore World Spirits Competition – Silver 2019, SIP Awards – Silver 2020, and NZ Spirits Awards – Silver 2019 & 20

Situated in New Plymouth's suburb of Westown near the start of Surf Highway 45, Begin Distilling is the home of Juno Gin. Following their three key values of "Make if Fun", "Make it Together", and "Make it Right" they engage with horticulturalists and researchers to locally source botanicals, and show their efficacy and flavour potential. They are also working with Massey University to create a world-first juniper plantation in New Zealand.

A classic style gin, Juno Extra Fine is their signature gin including a range of local botanicals.

GUIDE TO NEW ZEALAND GIN
— 2020 —
TASTERS'
PICK

GIN

Lighthouse Gin Original

42% ABV

DISTILLERY: Lighthouse Distillery, Martinborough
WEBSITE: lighthousegin.co.nz

BOTANICALS: Juniper, Coriander Seed, Yen Ben Lemon Zest, Navel Orange Zest, Cinnamon, Almond, Cassia Bark, Orris Root & Liquorice Root

---

TASTING NOTES: Aromatic juniper with zesty lemon and subtly sweet liquorice on the nose. Dry juniper led palate with cinnamon and orange. Lingering citrus and earthy spice developing on the finish.

SERVING SUGGESTION: Enjoy with Fever-Tree Premium Indian Tonic Water and a slice of lemon.

AWARDS: IWSC – Gold 2020, and Global Gin Masters - Master 90+ Points 2019

Located in the warm micro-climate of Martinborough in the Wairarapa that supports a thriving local agriculture and viticulture, Lighthouse Distillery is one of New Zealand's oldest craft gins. Taking inspiration from the region's iconic Cape Palliser Lighthouse and its association with craftsmanship, they only use the purest water filtered from high in the nearby Remutaka Ranges in their twice distilled gins.

A classic style gin, Lighthouse Gin Original's recipe was perfected over many years with a unique blend of nine botanicals and was the first ever New Zealand gin to be selected for presentation by the UK's Craft Gin Club.

RACHEL HALL
NEW ZEALAND
LIMITED EDITION
EST 95
HAND CRAFTED
LIGHTHOUSE
BATCH DISTILLED
GIN
SMALL / BATCH
DISTILLED AND BOTTLED
IN NEW ZEALAND
42% ALC/VOL 700 ML

Little Biddy Gin - Classic
40% ABV

DISTILLERY: Reefton Distilling Co., Reefton
VISIT THEM: 10 Smith Street, Reefton
WEBSITE: reeftondistillingco.com

BOTANICALS: Horopito, Tarata, Toatoa, Rimu, Douglas Fir, Angelica, Cardamom, Cassia, Coriander Seed, Lemon Peel, Juniper, Liquorice & Orris Root

---

TASTING NOTES: Fragrant lemon and distinctive peppery horopito aroma. Dry juniper palate followed by hints of cinnamon and sweet, savoury notes. Nutmeg and peppercorn emerge on the finish.

SERVING SUGGESTION: Enjoy with Fever-Tree Premium Indian Tonic Water and a slice of lemon.

AWARDS: San Francisco World Spirits Competition — Silver 2019 & Bronze 2020, NZ Spirits Awards — Bronze 2019 & 20, and SIP Awards — Gold 2020

Stationed deep in the Inangahua River Valley in the West Coast town of Reefton, Little Biddy is named in honour of the local legend Bridget 'Biddy' Goodwin, a pipe-smoking, gin-toting, 4-foot-tall gold prospector who lived in the 1800s. A modern distillery in an age-old town, Reefton Distilling Co. use large numbers of native botanicals from the surrounding rainforest to achieve a distinct West Coast flavour.

A classic style gin, Little Biddy Gin — Classic makes use of several native botanicals including toatoa, tarata, horopito, and rimu, as well as the majestic douglas fir which are all foraged locally prior to distillation.

BATCH №
20/001
SMALL BATCH
DISTILLED
LITTLE BIDDY®
New Zealand Botanical Gin
BOTANICALS
Toatoa + Horopito + Tarata + Rimu + Douglas Fir Tips + Juniper + Cassia + Angelica + Liquorice + Coriander + Orris Root + Cardamom + Fresh Lemon Peel
40% ABV | 700ml

Verdigris New Zealand Dry Gin

44% ABV

DISTILLERY: The National Distillery Company, Napier
VISIT THEM: 1 Ossian Street, Ahuriri, Napier
WEBSITE: nationaldistillery.nz

BOTANICALS: Juniper, Coriander Seed, Angelica Root, Cardamom, Orris Root, Cassia Bark, Lemon Peel, New Zealand Flax Seed & Liquorice Root

---

TASTING NOTES: Lifted juniper with fragrant orange and hints of aromatic spice on the nose. Dry palate with emerging notes of pepper, star anise, and earthy spice, followed by a clean juniper finish.

SERVING SUGGESTION: Enjoy with Fever-Tree Mediterranean Tonic Water and a slice of lemon.

AWARDS: Australian Gin Awards – Gold 2019 & Silver 2020, NZ Spirits Awards Bronze 2020, Sip Awards -Double Gold 2020, London Spirit Competition – Silver 2020, and Ultimate Beverage Challenge USA – Top 100 Spirits & 95 Points

Ensconced in the commercial-industrial northern waterfront of Napier, The National Distillery Company resides in one of the cities architectural crown jewels. Built in 1931 following the Napier earthquake, it reflects the influences of Art Nouveau and Modernism, or Art Deco, that were in vogue at the time. They blend modern distilling techniques with time-honoured traditions, looking to this duality to inspire their creativity and overall approach to gin making.

A classic style gin, Verdigris New Zealand Dry Gin is inspired by London Dry Gin and highlights native New Zealand flax seed among its botanicals.

VERDIGRIS
COPPER DISTILLED GIN
NEW ZEALAND
AOTEAROA
HAND CRAFTED FROM TIME HONOURED TRADITIONS

Reid + Reid Native Gin

42% ABV

DISTILLERY: Reid + Reid Distillery, Martinborough
VISIT THEM: 145 Todds Road, Martinborough
WEBSITE: reidandreid.co.nz

BOTANICALS: Juniper, Coriander Seed, Angelica Root, Licorice Root, Orris Root, Fennel Seed, Nutmeg, Cassia, Cardamom, Orange Peel, Kawakawa, Horopito & Manuka

---

TASTING NOTES: Aromatic juniper and sweet orange aroma. Dry palate with distinctive fresh orange, nutmeg, and spice. Earthy finish with lingering citrus.

SERVING SUGGESTION: Enjoy with Fever-Tree Mediterranean Tonic Water and a slice of lemon.

AWARDS: Do Not Compete

Based in the warm micro-climate of Martinborough in the Wairarapa that supports a thriving local agriculture and viticulture, Reid + Reid Distillery was founded in 2015 by two brothers with backgrounds in engineering and beverage production. They seek to challenge the perception of a 'classic' gin and promote New Zealand's unique native flora.

A classic style gin, Reid + Reid Native Gin is the result of a two year mission foraging the landscapes of New Zealand for the aromatic native plants that best compliment a classic dry gin, including kawakawa, manuka, and horopito.

· EST 2015 ·
NEW ZEALAND
REID+REID
NATIVE GIN
DISTILLED WITH NATIVE NEW ZEALAND BOTANICALS

Reid + Reid Rev. Dawson's Gin

42% ABV

DISTILLERY: Reid + Reid Distillery, Martinborough
VISIT THEM: 145 Todds Road, Martinborough
WEBSITE: reidandreid.co.nz

BOTANICALS: Juniper, Coriander Seed, Angelica Root, Orris Root, Fennel Seed, Cassia, Orange & Grapefruit

---

TASTING NOTES: Aromatic juniper with earthy root and orange peel on the nose. A clean and herbal palate with a hint of citrus and spice. Dry finish with lingering citrus and subtle fruity tones emerging.

SERVING SUGGESTION: Enjoy with Fever-Tree Premium Indian Tonic Water and a slice of grapefruit.

AWARDS: Do Not Compete

Based in the warm micro-climate of Martinborough in the Wairarapa that supports a thriving local agriculture and viticulture, Reid + Reid Distillery was founded in 2015 by two brothers with backgrounds in engineering and beverage production. They seek to challenge the perception of a 'classic' gin and promote New Zealand's unique native flora.

A classic style gin, Reid + Reid Rev. Dawson's Gin is distilled using the 'one shot' method and is named tongue-in-cheek after one of New Zealand's leading prohibitionists from the early 1900's who also happens to be the brothers' great, great grandfather.

EST 2015
R R
NEW ZEALAND
REID+REID
REV. DAWSON'S GIN
AN HOMAGE TO A NEW ZEALAND PROHIBITIONIST

Roots Marlborough Dry Gin

45% ABV

DISTILLERY: Elemental Distillers, Blenheim
VISIT THEM: 195 Rapaura Road, Rapaura, Blenheim
WEBSITE: elementaldistillers.com

BOTANICALS: Juniper, Grapefruit Zest, Coriander Seed, Organic Hops, Kawakawa Fruit & Gorse Flower

---

TASTING NOTES: Aromatic juniper with distinctive grapefruit and hoppy herbaceous aromas. Dry peppered juniper palate with spicy earth complexity leading into a long finish.

SERVING SUGGESTION: Enjoy with Fever-Tree Mediterranean Tonic Water and a slice of grapefruit.

AWARDS: NZ Spirits Awards – Gold 2020

Stationed out in the fertile Wairau Plain at the heart of the Marlborough wine region, Roots Marlborough Dry Gin creates small batches using a boutique 200 litre copper pot still and a sustainable neutral base spirit. They work closely with independent farmers, foragers, and cooperative to ensure that they get the finest quality botanicals from those who know and grow them best while striving for complete transparency, going from root to cup.

A classic style gin, Roots Marlborough Dry Gin is in the style of a London Dry Gin using New Zealand native and grown botanicals.

HAND
HARVESTED
BATCH
DISTILLED
MADE IN
NZ
ROOTS
MARLBOROUGH DRY GIN
700 ML
45% ALC/VOL

Scapegrace Classic

42.2% ABV

DISTILLERY: Scapegrace Distilling Co., Christchurch
WEBSITE: scapegracedistillery.com

BOTANICALS: Lemon Peel, Orage Peel, Corander Seed, Cardamom, Nutmeg, Juniper, Angelica Root, Liquorice Root, Orris Root, Cloves, Cinnamon & Cassia Bark

---

TASTING NOTES: A soft, subtle spice with lemon freshness on the nose. Dry palate with juniper and sweet lemon, finishing with lingering citrus and subtly spiced juniper.

SERVING SUGGESTION: Enjoy with Fever-Tree Premium Indian Tonic Water and a slice of orange.

AWARDS: San Francisco World Spirits Competition — Double Gold 2014, Gin Masters — Gold 2018 and London International Wines & Spirits Competition — Outstanding Silver 2014, Silver 2018 & Gold 2020

Tucked away in the 'Garden City' of Christchurch, Scapegrace Distilling Co. make their gin using glacial water that takes 80 years to filter through the rock of the Southern Alps before being released into an aquifer. They use a restored 19th century hand-beaten copper pot still to create their gins in the same way it was done back then. This is reflected in their bottles which are a modern take on the genever (Dutch gin) bottles from 200 years ago.

A classic style gin, Scapegrace Classic epitomises the nature of a classic gin, made using 12 botanicals of which juniper and citrus peel shine through.

BATCH:
0001
DISTILLED IN
NEW ZEALAND
N
SMALL PREMIUM BATCH
SCAPEGRACE
W E
DRY GIN
NEW ZEALAND
S
HANDCRAFTED
ARTISAN GIN
42.2% ABV
700ml

Solace Dry Gin

42.2% ABV

DISTILLERY: Kings Liquor, Auckland
WEBSITE: solacegin.co.nz

BOTANICALS: Juniper, Coriander Seed, Cassia Bark, Angelica Root, Nutmeg, Citrus Peel, Tangerine, Orris Root, Star Anise, Anise, Lemon, Orange & Cardamon

---

TASTING NOTES: Aromatic juniper with a hint of savoury root and subtle spice on the nose. Dry palate with juniper and emerging peppery spice, clean spicy finish with a touch of citrus.

SERVING SUGGESTION: Enjoy with Fever-Tree Premium Indian Tonic Water and a slice of lemon.

Huddled on the northern edge of Auckland in the suburb of Rosedale, Solace Gin is produced by Kings Liquor which has been making spirits since 1985. They produce small, handcrafted, artisanal batches of triple distilled gin which is echoed in their hand-illustrated labels that reflect the traditional crafting and blending of their recipes.

A classic style gin, Solace Dry Gin pays homage to the London Dry Gin style using a mixture of 13 traditional botanicals.

HAND CRAFTED
SOLACE
DRY GIN
PREMIUM
TRIPLE DISTILLED
London Dry
Small Batch infused
WITH 13 BOTANICALS
EXPERTLY
CRAFTED
KIN
EST.
700ML
BOTTLED IN NEW ZEALAND
42.2% ALC VOL

The Source Gin

47% ABV

DISTILLERY: The Cardrona Distillery, Cardrona
VISIT THEM: 2125 Cardrona Valley Road, Cardrona
WEBSITE: cardronadistillery.com

BOTANICALS: Juniper, Rosehip, Angelica Root, Coriander Seed, Lemon Zest & Orange Zest

---

TASTING NOTES: Floral rosehip and lifted lemon freshness on the nose. Earthy juniper on the palate with hints of candied fruit and zesty citrus. Subtle hints of spice emerging on the finish.

SERVING SUGGESTION: Enjoy with Fever-Tree Mediterranean Tonic Water and a slice of orange.

AWARDS: : New York World Wine & Spirits Competition — Gold 2016, and 'The Fifty Best' — Gold Medal 2017

Tucked up in the breath-taking Cardrona Valley between Wanaka and Queenstown, The Source Gin is produced on-site at The Cardrona Distillery. They use a single malt spirit in their two bespoke, handmade copper pot stills all the way from Scotland and abstain from chill-filtering in order to achieve a fuller flavour and character.

A classic style gin, The Source Gin includes locally foraged rosehip among their botanicals, which was first brought to the Cardrona Valley by Chinese immigrants during the gold rush.

CARDRONA DISTILLERY
THE
SOURCE
PURE CARDRONA GIN
47% ALC/VOL 750 ML
HAND-DISTILLED & BOTTLED IN NEW ZEALAND

Victor Gin Original
42% ABV

DISTILLERY: Thomson Whisky Distillery, Riverhead
WEBSITE: thomsonwhisky.com

BOTANICALS: Juniper, Lemon, Lemongrass, Cardamom & Coriander Seed

---

TASTING NOTES: Lifted and fragrant lemon freshness with a hint of cardamom on the nose. Dry palate with bursting cardamom and juniper, finishing with a clean, bold lemon freshness as the spice tapers off.

SERVING SUGGESTION: Enjoy with Fever-Tree Aromatic Tonic Water and a slice of lemon.

AWARDS: San Francisco World Spirits Competition – Double Gold 2019 and NZ Spirits Awards – Silver 2020

Based in the historic township of Riverhead to the north of Auckland, Victor Gin was born out of tinkering and experimentation at the Thomson Whisky Distillery. Taking inspiration from the world of music they focus on fresh botanicals and the heavy use of juniper to create the best spirits they can.

A classic style gin, Victor Gin Original looks to early rock n' roll and the idea of using only a few instruments that sound great together by using only the flavours that they love rather than a broad range of botanicals.

VICTOR GIN
HEAVY
BOTANICAL
NEW ZEALAND
ABV • 700 MLS
SAN FRANCISCO
WORLD
SPIRITS
COMPETITION
DOUBLE GOLD

Waitoki Gin

43% ABV

DISTILLERY: Washhouse Distillery, Waitoki

WEBSITE: washhousedistillery.co.nz

BOTANICALS: Juniper, Coriander Seed, Angelica Root, Orange, Grapefruit, Kawakawa, Horopito & a Secret Local Botanical

---

TASTING NOTES: Aromatic juniper with fruity grapefruit and zesty orange on the nose. Dry palate with bold juniper and hints of earthy root and peppery horopito. Fruity grapefruit emerges and carries through the finish.

SERVING SUGGESTION: Enjoy with Fever-Tree Aromatic Tonic Water and a slice of grapefruit.

AWARDS: NZ Spirits Awards – Silver 2020

Secluded amongst the many dairy farms that surround the small town of Waitoki to the north of Auckland, Washhouse Distillery makes small batches in a handmade copper alembic still from Portugal it what was once a home garage. They pride themselves on the manual nature of their process and lack of pretence.

A classic style gin, Waitoki Gin was born out of 40 different recipes over the course of 18 months, combining traditional botanicals with native kawakawa and horopito, fresh orange and grapefruit, and additions from a local tree that is 200+ years old.

FAMILY OWNED
& MADE
BY HAND
IN NZ
Waitoki
Washhouse
36°37'27"S 174°33'30"E
GIN
700ml
43% Alc/Vol

Wild Diamond Rare Dry Gin

42% ABV

DISTILLERY: Wild Diamond Distillery, Wanaka
WEBSITE: wilddiamond.co.nz

BOTANICALS: Juniper, Coriander Seed, Angelica Root, Cassia, Liquorice Extract, Cinnamon, Almond, Manuka, Rosehip, Elderflower, Lavender, Astragalus & Others Not Disclosed

---

TASTING NOTES: Aromatic juniper with complex earthy root characters on the nose. A bold, savoury palate with roasted nut and juniper, hints of spice and coriander emerge over a lingering dry finish.

SERVING SUGGESTION: Enjoy with Fever-Tree Aromatic Tonic Water, and a slice of lemon.

AWARDS: NZ Spirits Awards – Silver 2019

Sheltered between the foothills of the Southern Alps and Lake Wanaka, Wild Diamond Distillery takes its name from the natural elements that surround them. They select their botanicals based on their quality and character, sourcing them both internationally and locally. Maintaining their connection to their environment, their stills are powered by renewable wind and water energy, and they invest back into water and aquatic habitat enhancement, recovery, and restoration initiatives.

A classic style gin, Wild Diamond Rare Dry Gin is a limited edition premium batch with botanicals including manuka, rosehip, elderflower, lavender, and astragalus.

WILD DIAMOND
~ Rare Dry Gin ~
DISTILLER
BATCH 8
BOTTLE 004
HANDCRAFTED BOTANICAL GIN
DISTILLED IN WANAKA, NEW ZEALAND
750ml 42% alc./vol.

1919 Classic Gin

41% ABV

DISTILLERY: 1919 Distilling, Auckland
WEBSITE: 1919distilling.com

BOTANICALS: Juniper, Coriander Seed, Green Cardamom, Lemon Peel, Orange Peel, Angelica Root, Cherry, Manuka Honey & Cinnamon

---

TASTING NOTES: Bold aromatic juniper with coriander and lemon freshness on the nose. Crisp elegant palate with a hint of spice. Citrus and honey emerge over a dry clean finish.

SERVING SUGGESTION: Enjoy with Fever-Tree Premium Indian Tonic Water and a slice of lemon.

AWARDS: New Zealand Artisan Awards – Alcohol Category Winner 2019, Australian Gin Awards – Silver 2019, NZ Spirits Awards - Silver 2020, and SIP Awards – Bronze 2020

Nestled in the bustling industrial area of East Tamaki, 1919 Distilling prides itself on sourcing everything locally, even down to their custom made still, so that they can ensure the best quality and craftsmanship. Named for the year that New Zealand voted down prohibition they also stay true to the way gin was made in the 1900's by using ethanol made from cane sugar rather than whey.

A classic style gin, as its name suggests, the 1919 Classic Gin celebrates old world charm with botanicals like juniper, angelica root, and cinnamon in combination with Otago cherries, manuka honey, and organic lemons and oranges.

NZ MADE
1919
DISTILLING
GIN
Est. 2017
HAND-CRAFTED
SMALL BATCH
700ml
NEW ZEALAND MADE, DISTILLED & BOTTLED
ALC BY VOL 41%
82 PROOF

CONTEMPORARY

CONTAINING CONTEMPORARY GINS

Contemporary Gin – Gins that have a predominant flavour of anything other than juniper. Juniper is always present, but the overall character will emphasize the other botanicals over the juniper.

Ariki Ultra Premium Gin

45% ABV

DISTILLERY: Ariki Spirit, Riverhead
WEBSITE: arikispirit.com

BOTANICALS: Juniper, Almond, Coriander Seed, Angelica Root, Orange Peel, Orris Root, Lemon Peel, Liquorice Root, Black Pepper, Cardamom, Manuka Flower, Cinnamon, Lemon Grass, Vanilla & Coconut

---

TASTING NOTES: Aromatic juniper with aromas of sweet vanilla and almond. Firm palate with vanilla and citrus developing, subtle juniper notes on the finish.

SERVING SUGGESTION: Enjoy with Fever-Tree Mediterranean Tonic Water and a slice of lemon.

Tucked away in the historic township of Riverhead to the north of Auckland, Ariki Spirit distils their gin using a combination of their own custom-designed reflux method and vapour distillation with unique botanicals to achieve distinctive aromatic notes. Ariki means 'high chief' or 'leader' in Te Reo and is associated with carrying great prestige or mana and reflects their goal of bringing the Spirit of the Pacific to the world.

A contemporary style gin, Ariki Ultra Premium Gin is a smooth collaboration of pure New Zealand water and unique Pacific botanicals including Rarotongan vanilla and Tongan coconut.

ARIKI
SPIRIT OF THE
PACIFIC
Ultra Premium
GIN
DISTILLED WITH PURE
NEW ZEALAND WATER
700 mL

The Bureaucrat

41% ABV

DISTILLERY: Bureaucrats Gin Ltd., Wellington

WEBSITE: bureaucratsgin.co.nz

BOTANICALS: Juniper, Coriander Seed, Cinnamon
& Others Not Disclosed

TASTING NOTES: Aromatic cinnamon with prominent five spice and lifted lemon freshness. Cinnamon forward on the palate with a subtle hint of juniper, subtle citrus and mellow cinnamon bitterness on the finish.

SERVING SUGGESTION: Enjoy with Fever-Tree Aromatic Tonic Water and a slice of lemon.

AWARDS: NZ Spirits Awards – Silver 2020

Located in the windy capital city of Wellington, Bureaucrats Gin Ltd. was started by two bureaucrats with the hobby of distilling gin in their home laundries. Driven by a love of fine gin and fine things, they used the age old method of trial and error until they had developed a distillation consistency and quality which they could share with the world. Producing small batches, they focus on innovation and bold botanical combinations.

A contemporary gin, The Bureaucrat has a combination of ten botanicals with bold flavours of spice and sweet undertones.

BUREAUCRATS GIN

THE
BUREAUCRAT
AWARDED
SILVER
New Zealand
Spirits Awards
2019
WELLINGTON
GIN
DISTILLED AND BOTTLED BY HAND
Batch no: 0036
70CL
A GIN OF 10 FINE
BOTANICALS
WITH AN AUDACIOUS
CINNAMON HIT
41% ALC. VOL.

The Doyenne

41% ABV

DISTILLERY: Bureaucrats Gin Ltd., Wellington

WEBSITE: bureaucratsgin.co.nz

BOTANICALS: Juniper, Coriander Seed, Coconut, Lime, Lemongrass & Others Not Disclosed

---

TASTING NOTES: Aromatic lime and sweet lemongrass with a hint of creamed honey on the nose. Bold lemongrass and juniper across the palate, finishing with a hint of coconut cream.

SERVING SUGGESTION: Enjoy with Fever-Tree Aromatic Tonic Water and a slice of lime.

AWARDS: NZ Spirits Awards – Gold 2020

Located in the windy capital city of Wellington, Bureaucrats Gin Ltd. was started by two bureaucrats with the hobby of distilling gin in their home laundries. Driven by a love of fine gin and fine things, they used the age old method of trial and error until they had developed a distillation consistency and quality which they could share with the world. Producing small batches, they focus on innovation and bold botanical combinations.

A contemporary gin, The Doyenne uses a unique combination of botanicals, including coconut, lime, and zesty lemongrass.

BUREAUCRATS GIN

THE
DOYENNE
WELLINGTON
GIN
DISTILLED AND BOTTLED BY HAND
Batch no: 0025
70CL
BUREAUCRATS
GIN LTD
41% ALC. VOL.

The Bond Store Kawakawa Gin

37.5% ABV

DISTILLERY: Koakoa, Paraparaumu

VISIT THEM: 3c Magrath Avenue, Paraparaumu Beach

WEBSITE: koakoa.nz

BOTANICALS: Not Disclosed

TASTING NOTES: Delicate lemongrass and kawakawa aroma on the nose. Clean, dry palate with soft juniper and citrus, finishing with a gentle herbal lemon freshness.

SERVING SUGGESTION: Enjoy with Fever-Tree Mediterranean Tonic Water and a slice of lemon.

AWARDS: NZ Spirits Awards – Bronze 2019 and Cathy Pacific Hong Kong International Wine and Spirit Competition – Bronze 2019

Situated just a couple of minutes away from the Paraparaumu Beach shoreline on the spectacular Kapiti Coast, The Bond Store is produced by Koakoa (which means 'happiness' in Te Reo) a liqueur and spirits distiller, and named after the old bond accredited alcohol taxation system. They use sustainable New Zealand ingredients and whey spirit to handcraft their gin which is the result of a lot of research and experimentation with several recipes.

A contemporary gin, The Bond Store Kawakawa Gin is made using a unique selection of botanicals including kawakawa grown on the family farm in rural Wairarapa.

EST. 2018
THE
BOND
STORE
MADE IN NEW ZEALAND
KAWAKAWA
GIN

Curiosity Gin - Recipe #23

42% ABV

DISTILLERY: The Spirits Workshop Distillery, Christchurch
VISIT THEM: 11 Sandyford Street, Sydenham, Christchurch
WEBSITE: thespiritsworkshop.co.nz

BOTANICALS: Juniper, Manuka Berries & Leaves, Coriander Seed, Cardamom, Orange Zest, Lime Zest, Ginger Root, Angelica Root, Lavender, Cinnamon & Star Anise

---

TASTING NOTES: Soft fragrant aromas of sweet spice, zesty citrus, and floral undertones. Clean and dry on the palate with very subtle juniper and hints of citrus. Powerful finish with earthy spice and nutty root characters.

SERVING SUGGESTION: Enjoy with Fever-Tree Mediterranean Tonic Water and a slice of pink grapefruit.

AWARDS: Monde Awards — Gold 2017, San Francisco World Spirits Competition — Bronze 2018, SIP Awards — Silver 2018, and NZ Spirits Awards — Bronze 2020

Established in the light industrial area of Christchurch's suburb Sydenham, Curiosity Gin set out from the start to create truly unique and individual gins that stand out from the crowd and the tonic. To hold true to these values their gins are made "grain to glass" where possible, in small batches using their copper pot still.

A contemporary gin, Curiosity Gin - Recipe #23 is made using a base spirit distilled in-house from Canterbury malted barley and 11 botanicals including a generous helping of East Coast manuka, fresh citrus, and Otago lavender.

GUIDE TO NEW ZEALAND GIN
— 2020 —
TASTERS' PICK

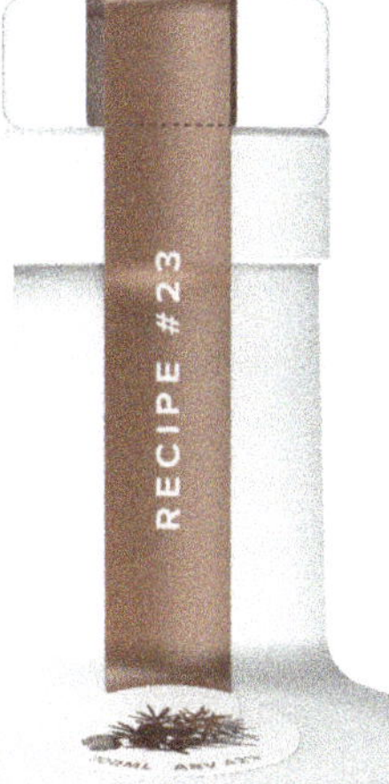

RECIPE #23

CURIOSITY GIN
GIN
CURIOSITY

Denzien Smoke & Embers Gin

44% ABV

DISTILLERY: Denzien Urban Distillery, Wellington
VISIT THEM: 10 Lombard Street, Te Aro, Wellington
WEBSITE: denzien-urban-distillery.business.site

BOTANICALS: Juniper, Morita, Chipotle, Guajillo, California, Mulato Negro & Habanero Chillies, Coriander Seed, Angelica Root, Fennel Seed, Liquorice Root & Orris Root

---

TASTING NOTES: Aromatic juniper with earthy smoke and a hint of chilli on the nose. Juniper leads with soft chilli notes emerging, finishing with an earthy spice and touch of warmth.

SERVING SUGGESTION: Enjoy with Fever-Tree Smoked Ginger Ale and a slice of orange.

Standing in the heart of Wellington's vibrant central Te Aro suburb, Denzien Urban Distillery is an artisan gin distillery with a mission to make brazen city gins for city people. They produce small batches in their handmade copper pot still and use distilled rainwater, all of which can be watched in person before tasting at their visitable location.

A contemporary gin, Denzien Smoke & Embers Gin is designed to mimic some of the qualities of whiskey by including morita, chipotle, and habanero as botanicals.

HAND CRAFTED IN WELLINGTON
DENZIEN
URBAN DISTILLERY
SMALL GIN BATCH
OF NEW ZEALAND
700ml
44%ABV
SMOKE & EMBERS
UNASHAMEDLY URBAN GIN

Dr Beak

Dr Beak New Zealand Premium Gin

48% ABV

DISTILLERY: Elemental Distillers, Blenheim
VISIT THEM: 195 Rapaura Road, Rapaura, Blenheim
WEBSITE: drbeak.nz

BOTANICALS: Juniper, Coriander Seed, Lavender, Mint, Chamomile, Lemon Verbena, Orris Root, Thyme, Rosemary, Lime Peel, Kelp, Horopito & Bay Leaf

---

TASTING NOTES: Very aromatic and complex with hints of mint, lime, and lavender on the nose. Juniper-forward palate with herbal rosemary and horopito. Long earthy notes with zesty lime and floral sweetness on the finish.

SERVING SUGGESTION: Enjoy with Fever-Tree Mediterranean Tonic Water and a sprig of rosemary.

Based in the warm micro-climate of Martinborough in the Wairarapa but distilled in Blenheim, Dr Beak took three years of recipe development to reach where they are now. Each botanical they use, except juniper, has been carefully selected based on their ability to be grown in New Zealand, with the aim of one day creating a gin from single site grown botanicals. With environmentalism at their core, they also donate 5% of their profits to Forest & Bird.

A contemporary gin, Dr Beak New Zealand Premium Gin is bursting with flavour due to the high number of essential oils and will proudly cloud up when left in the freezer or mixed with tonic.

BATCH
DISTILLED
Dr Beak
48%
ALC/VOL
NEW ZEALAND PREMIUM GIN
Bottles for
BIODIVERSITY

The Artist

40% ABV

DISTILLERY: Fenton Street Distillery, Stratford
VISIT THEM: 11 Fenton St, Stratford (by appointment)
WEBSITE: fentonartscollective.co.nz/distillery

BOTANICALS: Juniper, Coriander Seed, Cassia Bark, Nutmeg, Ginger, Horopito, Pepper & Kawakawa

---

TASTING NOTES: Bold aromatic juniper with lemon zest and herbaceous aroma. Dry lemon tarata freshness on the palate with peppery horopito and juniper. Subtle sweet honey notes and lemon finish.

SERVING SUGGESTION: Enjoy with Fever-Tree Mediterranean Tonic Water and a slice of lemon.

Huddled beneath the slopes of Mt Taranaki in the town of Stratford which is full of Shakespearian references, like many of their gins, Fenton Street Distillery has grown out of its founders' restoration of their 1920s neo-classical building. They are one of the smallest commercial distilleries in New Zealand, making deliberately small 48 litre batches to achieve a genuinely handcrafted product.

A contemporary gin, The Artist is triple distilled with horopito and ginger alongside five other botanicals to produce a gin that appeals to whiskey drinkers.

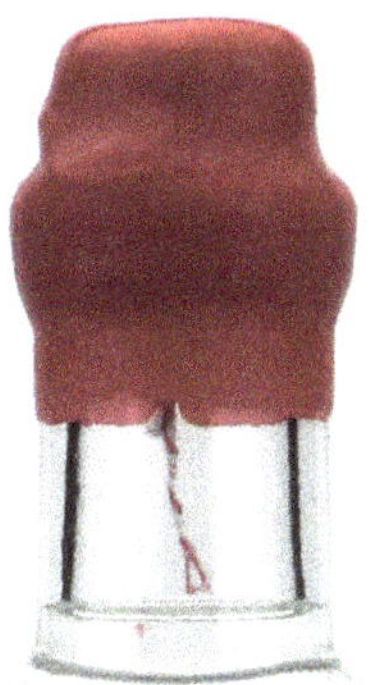

Fenton Street Distillery
Est. 2018
Stratford
New Zealand

IGNORE CLICHÉS
BE ORIGINAL
Genuinely Handcrafted
in very small batches
... for Gin's sake!
Est 2018
THE ARTIST
FENTON ST GIN
Fenton St Arts Collective Stratford

The Novelist

40% ABV

DISTILLERY: Fenton Street Distillery, Stratford
VISIT THEM: 11 Fenton St, Stratford (by appointment)
WEBSITE: fentonartscollective.co.nz/distillery

BOTANICALS: Juniper, Angelica, Coriander Seed, Horopito, Cassia Bark, Bush Honey, Orris, Almonds, Liquorice & Lime

---

TASTING NOTES: Aromatic juniper with fresh lime and hints of almond and pear on the nose. Peppery horopito is distinctive on the palate with a touch of lime and juniper. Dry finish with subtle oriental spice and slight floral undertones.

SERVING SUGGESTION: Enjoy with Fever-Tree Mediterranean Tonic Water and a slice of lime.

AWARDS: NZ Spirits Awards — Bronze 2020

Huddled beneath the slopes of Mt. Taranaki in the town of Stratford which is full of Shakespearian references, like many of their gins, Fenton Street Distillery has grown out of its founders' restoration of their 1920s neo-classical building. They are one of the smallest commercial distilleries in New Zealand, making deliberately small 48 litre batches to achieve a genuinely handcrafted product.

A contemporary gin, The Novelist uses bush honey from eastern Taranaki to draw together its other botanicals into a smooth yet complex gin.

Fenton Street Distillery
Est 2018
Stratford
New Zealand
IGNORE CLICHÉS
BE ORIGINAL
Genuinely Handcrafted
In very small batches
... for Gin's sake!
Est 2018
THE NOVELIST

FENTON ST GIN
Fenton St Arts Collective Stratford

The Poet

40% ABV

DISTILLERY: Fenton Street Distillery, Stratford
VISIT THEM: 11 Fenton St, Stratford (by appointment)
WEBSITE: fentonartscollective.co.nz/distillery

BOTANICALS: Juniper, Coriander Seed, Angelica, Orange Zest, Lime Zest, Cardamom & Orris Root

---

TASTING NOTES: Aromatic juniper with aromas of cardamom and zesty citrus. Dry palate with spicy angelica and bursting zesty citrus. Spicy peppery finish with a hint of juniper.

SERVING SUGGESTION: Enjoy with Fever-Tree Mediterranean Tonic Water and a slice of lemon.

Huddled beneath the slopes of Mt. Taranaki in the town of Stratford which is full of Shakespearian references, like many of their gins, Fenton Street Distillery has grown out of its founders' restoration of their 1920s neo-classical building. They are one of the smallest commercial distilleries in New Zealand, making deliberately small 48 litre batches to achieve a genuinely handcrafted product.

A contemporary gin, The Poet celebrates the traditional character of a London Dry Gin with the inclusion of New Zealand citruses.

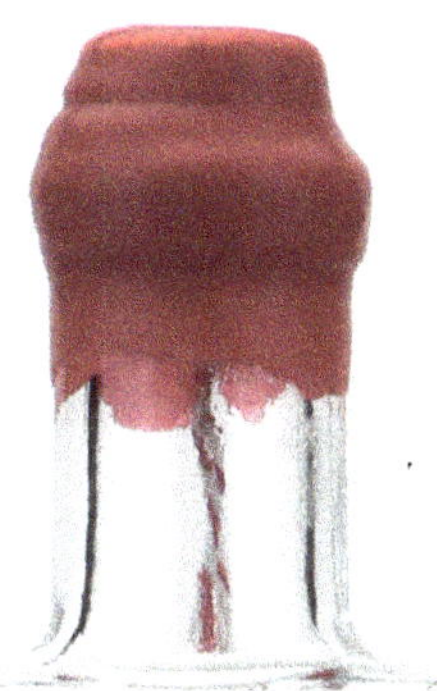

Street D
IGNORE CLICHÉS
BE ORIGINAL
Est 2018
Genuinely Handcrafted
In very small batches
Stratford
... for Gin's sake!
New Z
Est 2018
THE POET
FENTON ST GIN
40%
Fenton St Arts Collective Stratford

The Vintner

46% ABV

DISTILLERY: Fenton Street Distillery, Stratford

VISIT THEM: 11 Fenton St, Stratford (by appointment)

WEBSITE: fentonartscollective.co.nz/distillery

BOTANICALS: Juniper, Coriander Seed, Tarata, Horopito, Nutmeg, Oak Staves, Lemon Zest, Cassia Bark, Pepper, Bush Honey, Angelica & Kawakawa

---

TASTING NOTES: Bold aromatic juniper with lemon zest and herbaceous aroma. Dry lemon tarata freshness on the palate with peppery horopito and juniper. Subtle sweet honey notes and lemon finish.

SERVING SUGGESTION: Enjoy with Fever-Tree Mediterranean Tonic Water and a slice of lemon.

AWARDS: NZ Spirits Awards — Bronze 2020

Huddled beneath the slopes of Mt. Taranaki in the town of Stratford which is full of Shakespearian references, like many of their gins, Fenton Street Distillery has grown out of its founders' restoration of their 1920s neo-classical building. They are one of the smallest commercial distilleries in New Zealand, making deliberately small 48 litre batches to achieve a genuinely handcrafted product.

A contemporary gin, The Vintner showcases tannins from oak staves that are immersed in red wine for 24 months before distillation.

386
FENTON STREET
GIN
Est.2018
THE
VINTNER

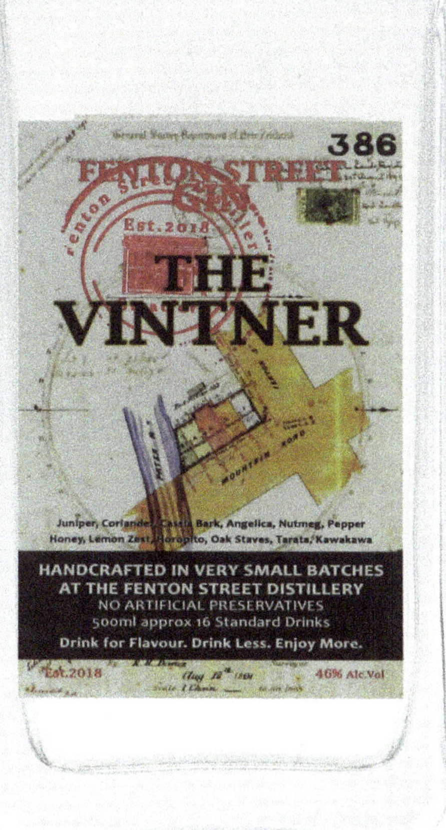
Juniper, Coriander, Cassia Bark, Angelica, Nutmeg, Pepper
Honey, Lemon Zest, Horopito, Oak Staves, Tarata, Kawakawa
HANDCRAFTED IN VERY SMALL BATCHES
AT THE FENTON STREET DISTILLERY
NO ARTIFICIAL PRESERVATIVES
500ml approx 16 Standard Drinks
Drink for Flavour. Drink Less. Enjoy More.
Est.2018
46% Alc.Vol

Grey Lynn Gin

40% ABV

DISTILLERY: Grey Lynn Gin Distillery, Auckland

WEBSITE: greylynngin.com

BOTANICALS: Juniper, Fennel Seed, Orange Peel
& a Secret Local Botanical

TASTING NOTES: Sweet bubblegum candy aroma with a hint of spice on the nose. A bold palate with sweet candy flavours and subtle notes of juniper, finishing with a light zesty orange freshness.

SERVING SUGGESTION: Enjoy with Fever-Tree Premium Indian Tonic Water and a slice of orange.

Nestled in the charming central Auckland suburb of Grey Lynn, Grey Lynn Gin is one of the latest New Zealand distillers to enter the market. Started at the beginning of the year after being conceived on New Year's Eve, they've only just arrived on shelves in September. Handcrafted in a local garage, all of their distillation, bottling, and labelling is done by hand.

A contemporary gin, Grey Lynn Gin came about as the result of an intense trial and error process and includes a secret local ingredient.

GIN
DISTILLED
& BOTTLED
BY HAND
GREY LYNN
GREY
LYNN
GIN

20 SMALL BATCH 20
LOCALLY DISTILLED & HANDCRAFTED
GREY
LYNN
GIN
40% ALC/VOL
375 mL
N MADE IN GREY LYNN, NEW ZEALAND S

East Block 200

40% ABV

DISTILLERY: Hastings Distillers, Hastings
VISIT THEM: 231 Heretaunga Street East, Hastings
WEBSITE: hastingsdistillers.com

BOTANICALS: Juniper, Coriander Seed, Angelica Root, Orange Peel, Lemon Peel, Kaffir Lime Peel, Cassia Bark, Feijoa Leaf, Bay Leaf & Lavender

---

TASTING NOTES: Aromatic kaffir lime and lemongrass with subtle pepper and floral lavender on the nose. Light, clean palate with fresh citrus and a hint of root spice on the finish.

SERVING SUGGESTION: Enjoy with Fever-Tree Mediterranean Tonic Water and a kaffir lime leaf.

AWARDS: NZ Spirits Awards — Silver 2020

Situated near the edge of central Hastings in the fertile alluvial Heretaunga Plains, Hastings Distillers was New Zealand's first organic certified producer of spirits and liqueurs. They endeavour to grow as many of their botanicals as possible in the Hawke's Bay using organic and biodynamic practices, with the belief that the region's 'terroir' imprints on all of the botanicals. Once distilled they cut to strength using spring water from the nearby Kaweka Ranges.

A contemporary gin, East Block 200 contains ten organic botanicals of which nine are grown in Hawke's Bay.

EAST BLOCK 200
GIN
HASTINGS DISTILLERS
NEW ZEALAND

Albertine

47% ABV

DISTILLERY: Hastings Distillers, Hastings
VISIT THEM: 231 Heretaunga Street East, Hastings
WEBSITE: hastingsdistillers.com

BOTANICALS: Juniper, Coriander Seed, Angelica, Lime Peel, Lemon Peel, Orange Peel, Kaffir Lime Leaf & Peel, Grapefruit Peel, Lemon Verbena, Lemongrass, Lavender, Chamomile, Manuka Flower, Sage, Rosemary, 5 Exotic Peppers, Mace & Selected Spices

---

TASTING NOTES: Bold fruity aromatic juniper with layers of ripe citrus on the nose. Dry fresh lemon palate with a hint of chamomile and liquorice. Clean finish with lime and a delicate peppery spice that lingers.

SERVING SUGGESTION: Enjoy with Fever-Tree Mediterranean Tonic Water and a slice of lime.

AWARDS: NZ Spirits Awards – Silver 2020 and IWSC Spirit – Gold 2020

Situated near the edge of central Hastings in the fertile alluvial Heretaunga Plains, Hastings Distillers was New Zealand's first organic certified producer of spirits and liqueurs. They endeavour to grow as many of their botanicals as possible in the Hawkes Bay using organic and biodynamic practices, with the belief that the region's 'terroir' imprints on all of the botanicals. Once distilled they cut to strength using spring water from the nearby Kaweka Ranges.

A contemporary gin, Albertine contains 38 organic botanicals with the goal of creating a sensory landscape of the freshness and vibrancy of New Zealand.

RA ENIM ES
ALBERTINE
GIN
NATURE IS THE MEASURE
CREATED IN ACCORDANCE WITH THE LAWS OF NATURE AND FINE TUNED
BY OUR YEARS OF WINEMAKING, ALBERTINE IS A UNIQUE ARRANGEMENT
OF 56 WILD FORAGED, ORGANICALLY OR BIODYNAMICALLY GROWN
BOTANICALS, PURE ORGANIC SPIRIT AND LIVING WATER. SHAPED
AFTER EXPLORING OVER 300 FRUITS, ROOTS, LEAVES AND FLOWERS. IT IS
A SENSORY IMAGE OF OUR DISTINCT LANDSCAPE.
HASTINGS DISTILLERS
NEW ZEALAND

Original Island Gin

43.2% ABV

DISTILLERY: Island Gin Distillery, Great Barrier Island

WEBSITE: islandgin.com

BOTANICALS: Juniper, Manuka & Bush Honey, Coriander Seed, Lemon Myrtle & Others Not Disclosed

---

TASTING NOTES: Light juniper with zesty orange and toasted coriander on the nose. A clean palate with lemon freshness, bold juniper and a subtle creaminess. Dry finish with a hint of citrus persisting.

SERVING SUGGESTION: Enjoy with Fever-Tree Refreshingly Light Indian Tonic Water and a slice of lemon.

AWARDS: NZ Spirits Awards – Bronze 2020

Secreted away on the remote but beautiful Great Barrier Island, Island Gin Distillery has a sustainable ethos towards producing their small batch gins. Their bottles are designed to reflect a Kina shell and are made with almost 50% reclaimed glass, meaning that just like no two kina shells are alike, neither are their bottles. All of their gins are distilled in small batches using a copper still before heading to their solar-powered bottling line.

A contemporary gin, Original Island Gin is focused on the inclusion of Great Barrier Island manuka & bush honey.

43.2% ABV
700ml
Original
Small batch
distilled with
Great Barrier
Island Manuka
ISLAND
GIN
GT
BARRIER
ISL
N
Z

Black Label Tangelo Blossom Island Gin

46% ABV

DISTILLERY: Island Gin Distillery, Great Barrier Island

WEBSITE: islandgin.com

BOTANICALS: Juniper, Manuka & Bush Honey, Coriander Seed, Lemon Myrtle, Tangelo Blossoms & Others Not Disclosed

---

TASTING NOTES: Lifted juniper with bursting notes of lemon myrtle and delicate bush honey on the nose. Clean, dry palate with juniper and bold lemon freshness. Herbaceous earthy tones and honey sweetness on the finish.

SERVING SUGGESTION: Enjoy with Fever-Tree Mediterranean Tonic Water and a slice of tangelo.

AWARDS: NZ Spirits Awards – Bronze 2020

Secreted away on the remote but beautiful Great Barrier Island, Island Gin Distillery has a sustainable ethos towards producing their small batch gins. Their bottles are designed to reflect a Kina shell and are made with almost 50% reclaimed glass, meaning that just like no two kina shells are alike, neither are their bottles. All of their gins are distilled in small batches using a copper still before heading to their solar-powered bottling line.

A contemporary gin, Black Label Tangelo Blossom Island Gin is made using tangelos grown on the island which are steeped in their original gin before being redistilled with tangelo blossoms and other island grown botanicals.

46% ABV
700ml
Tangelo
Small batch
distilled with
Great Barrier
ISLAND
GT
BARRIER
ISL
N Z
GIN

Juno Summer 2020 Seasonal Gin

44% ABV

DISTILLERY: Begin Distilling, New Plymouth

VISIT THEM: 16 Sunley Street, Westown, New Plymouth

WEBSITE: junogin.com

BOTANICALS: Juniper, Coriander Seed, Angelica Root, Orris Root, Manuka, Orange Black Peppercorns, Cardamom, Cassia, Rosehip & Rose Petals

---

TASTING NOTES: Aromatic rose and fresh orange peel on the nose. A clean juniper palate and spice emerging throughout, followed by honey sweetness and floral rosehip finish.

SERVING SUGGESTION: Enjoy with Fever-Tree Elderflower Tonic Water and a slice of orange.

AWARDS: NZ Spirits Awards – Silver 2020

Situated in New Plymouth's suburb of Westown near the start of Surf Highway 45, Begin Distilling is the home of Juno Gin. Following their three key values of "Make if Fun", "Make it Together", and "Make it Right" they engage with horticulturalists and researchers to locally source botanicals, and show their efficacy and flavour potential.

A contemporary gin, Juno Summer 2020 Gin is a seasonal gin focusing on the inclusion of floral flavours like rosehip and rose petals, a maximum of only 1000 bottles are produced each year.

JUNO
BIG NOSE SEASONAL GIN
SUMMER
200ml 44.6% Alc/Vol

Juno Autumn 2020 Seasonal Gin
44% ABV

DISTILLERY: Begin Distilling, New Plymouth
VISIT THEM: 16 Sunley Street, Westown, New Plymouth
WEBSITE: junogin.com

BOTANICALS: Juniper, Coriander Seed, Angelica Root, Orris Root, Manuka, Orange, Black Peppercorns, Cardamom, Cassia, Cinnamon & Horopito

---

TASTING NOTES: Aromatic juniper with fragrant notes of lemon-honey and zesty orange on the nose. A clean palate of peppery horopito and emerging rose. Dry citrus finish with a hint of autumn spice.

SERVING SUGGESTION: Enjoy with Fever-Tree Spiced Orange Ginger Ale and a slice of orange.

AWARDS: NZ Spirits Awards – Silver 2020

Situated in New Plymouth's suburb of Westown near the start of Surf Highway 45, Begin Distilling is the home of Juno Gin. Following their three key values of "Make if Fun", "Make it Together", and "Make it Right" they engage with horticulturalists and researchers to locally source botanicals and show their efficacy and flavour potential.

A contemporary gin, Juno Autumn 2020 Gin is a seasonal gin focusing on the inclusion of citrus and Autumn spices, a maximum of only 1000 bottles are produced each year.

juno
AUTUMN
200ml 44.0% Alc/Vol

Juno Winter 2020 Seasonal Gin

44% ABV

DISTILLERY: Begin Distilling, New Plymouth
VISIT THEM: 16 Sunley Street, Westown, New Plymouth
WEBSITE: junogin.com

BOTANICALS: Juniper, Coriander Seed, Angelica Root, Orris Root, Manuka, Orange, Black Peppercorns, Cardamom, Cassia, Cinnamon, Cloves, All Spice, Ginger, Rhubarb & Quince

---

TASTING NOTES: Aromatic dried fruit with hints of rhubarb, lemon and coriander on the nose. Dry palate delivering a subtle juniper, candied orange, and rhubarb. Christmas spice emerging for a bold finish.

SERVING SUGGESTION: Enjoy with Fever-Tree Mediterranean Tonic Water and a slice of orange.

AWARDS: NZ Spirits Awards – Bronze 2020

Situated in New Plymouth's suburb of Westown near the start of Surf Highway 45, Begin Distilling is the home of Juno Gin. Following their three key values of "Make if Fun", "Make it Together", and "Make it Right" they engage with horticulturalists and researchers to locally source botanicals and show their efficacy and flavour potential.

A contemporary gin, Juno Winter 2020 Gin is a seasonal gin focusing on the inclusion of classic Christmas spices, a maximum of only 1000 bottles are produced each year.

juno
LIMITED EDITION
SEASONAL GIN
2020
W I N T E R
200ml 44.0% Alc/Vol

Juno Sping 2020 Seasonal Gin

44% ABV

DISTILLERY: Begin Distilling, New Plymouth
VISIT THEM: 16 Sunley Street, Westown, New Plymouth
WEBSITE: junogin.com

BOTANICALS: Juniper, Coriander Seed, Angelica Root, Orris Root, Manuka, Orange, Pink Peppercorns, Cardamom, Cassia, Parsley Seed, Celery Seed, Dill Seed & Fennel Seed

---

TASTING NOTES: Aromatic juniper with fennel and a lemon-coriander freshness on the nose. Dry palate with dominating earthy root flavours and bold spice. Zesty lemon and lingering spice on the finish.

SERVING SUGGESTION: Enjoy with Fever-Tree Mediterranean Tonic Water and a slice of lemon.

AWARDS: NZ Spirits Awards – Gold 2020

Situated in New Plymouth's suburb of Westown near the start of Surf Highway 45, Begin Distilling is the home of Juno Gin. Following their three key values of "Make if Fun", "Make it Together", and "Make it Right" they engage with horticulturalists and researchers to locally source botanicals, and show their efficacy and flavour potential.

A contemporary gin, Juno Spring 2020 Gin is a seasonal gin focusing on the inclusion of herbal and earthy flavours like fennel, celery, parsley, and dill seeds, a maximum of only 1000 bottles are produced each year.

Juno
SPRING
2020
200ml 14.0% Alc/Vol

REEFTON
DISTILLING Co

WEST COAST—NEW ZEALAND
EST? 2017

Little Biddy Gin - Gold Label
43% ABV

DISTILLERY: Reefton Distilling Co., Reefton
VISIT THEM: 10 Smith Street, Reefton
WEBSITE: reeftondistillingco.com

BOTANICALS: Angelica Root, Caramelised Bears Limes, Cassia, Coriander Seed, Juniper, Kahikatea, Liquorice Root, Nutmeg, Orris Root, Pink Peppercorns, Snow Moss, Toatoa & Watercress

---

TASTING NOTES: Bold earthy aroma with kahikatea tips and a hint of fresh lime on the nose. Dry palate with herbaceous hints of spice. A subtle sweet lemon emerges on the finish.

SERVING SUGGESTION: Enjoy with Fever-Tree Mediterranean Tonic Water and a slice of lemon.

AWARDS: NZ Spirits Awards — Bronze 2019

Stationed deep in the Inangahua River Valley in the West Coast town of Reefton, Little Biddy is named in honour of the local legend Bridget 'Biddy' Goodwin, a pipe-smoking, gin-toting, 4-foot-tall gold prospector who lived in the 1800s. A modern distillery in an age-old town, Reefton Distilling Co. use large numbers of native botanicals from the surrounding rainforest to achieve a distinct West Coast flavour.

A contemporary gin, Little Biddy Gin — Gold Label is characterised by its use of local grain spirit, wild water, and hand harvested native botanicals including foraged watercress, snow moss, kahikatea tips, and toatoa.

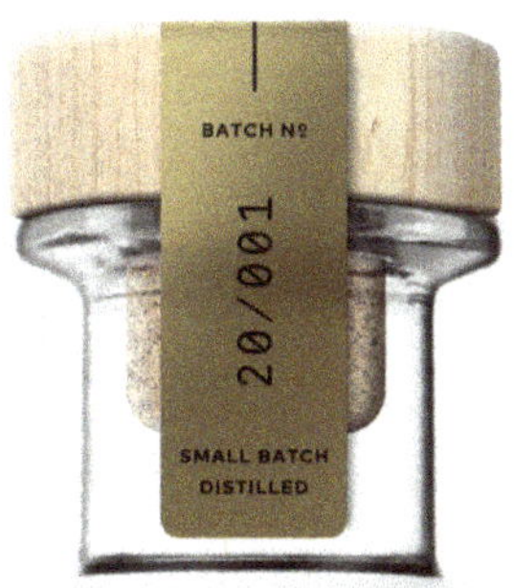
BATCH Nº
20/001
SMALL BATCH
DISTILLED
LITTLE BIDDY®
New Zealand Botanical Gin
GRAIN TO GLASS
WEST COAST
BOTANICAL DRY GIN
Kahikatea Tips + Toatoa +
Snow Moss + Watercress +
Juniper + Coriander + Cassia
+ Liquorice + Angelica + Lime
+ Orris Root + Nutmeg +
Pink Peppercorns
Handcrafted + Small Batch Distilled
Bottled in Reefton, West Coast, New Zealand
43% ABV | 700ml

REEFTON
DISTILLING Co

WEST COAST—NEW ZEALAND
ESTᴰ 2017

Little Biddy Gin - Black Label
46% ABV

DISTILLERY: Reefton Distilling Co., Reefton
VISIT THEM: 10 Smith Street, Reefton
WEBSITE: reeftondistillingco.com

BOTANICALS: Angelica Root, Caramelised Bears Limes, Cassia, Coriander Seed, Juniper, Kahikatea, Liquorice Root, Nutmeg, Orris Root, Pink Peppercorns, Snow Moss, Toatoa & Watercress

---

TASTING NOTES: : Bold earthy aroma with kahikatea tips and a hint of fresh lime on the nose. Earthy palate with herbal, savoury and rich complexities. Subtly sweet earthy finish with a touch of spice.

SERVING SUGGESTION: Enjoy neat or with Fever-Tree Mediterranean Tonic Water and a slice of lemon.

AWARDS: NZ Spirits Awards — Bronze 2019 and San Francisco World Spirits Competition — Bronze Medal 2019

Stationed deep in the Inangahua River Valley in the West Coast town of Reefton, Little Biddy is named in honour of the local legend Bridget 'Biddy' Goodwin, a pipe-smoking, gin-toting, 4-foot-tall gold prospector who lived in the 1800s. A modern distillery in an age-old town, Reefton Distilling Co. use large numbers of native botanicals from the surrounding rainforest to achieve a distinct West Coast flavour.

A contemporary gin, Little Biddy Gin — Black Label uses the same botanicals as their Gold Label but is designed as a sipping gin with a slightly higher alcohol content.

BATCH Nº
20/001
SMALL BATCH
DISTILLED
LITTLE BIDDY
New Zealand Botanical Gin
GRAIN TO GLASS
BLACK LABEL
DRY GIN
Kahikatea Tips + Toatoa +
Snow Moss + Watercress +
Juniper + Coriander + Cassia
+ Liquorice + Angelica + Lime
+ Orris Root + Nutmeg +
Pink Peppercorns
Handcrafted + Small Batch Distilled
Bottled in Reefton, West Coast, New Zealand
46% ABV | 700ml

Adorn Beauty Gin

42% ABV

DISTILLERY: The National Distillery, Napier

VISIT THEM: 1 Ossian Street, Ahuriri, Napier

WEBSITE: nationaldistillery.nz

BOTANICALS: Juniper, Coriander Seed, Angelica Root, Cardamom, Orris Root, Cassia Bark, Lemon Peel, Rosehip, Rose Petals, Chamomile, New Zealand Flax Seed & Liquorice Root

---

TASTING NOTES: Aromatic juniper with floral lemon and earthy complexity on the nose. Dry palate with notable juniper, finishing with lingering citrus peel and light peppery spice.

SERVING SUGGESTION: Enjoy with Fever-Tree Refreshingly Light Indian Tonic Water and a slice of lemon.

AWARDS: Australian Gin Awards – Silver 2019 & 20, The Junipers New Zealand Gin Awards – Silver 2020, Cathay Pacific International Wine and Spirit Competition – Bronze 2019, New York World Wine & Spirits Competition – Bronze 2019, and Ultimate Beverage Challenge USA – 92 Points 2020

Ensconced in the commercial-industrial northern waterfront of Napier, The National Distillery Company resides in one of the cities architectural crown jewels. Built in 1931 following the Napier earthquake, it reflects the influences of Art Nouveau and Modernism, or Art Deco, that were in vogue at the time. They blend modern distilling techniques with time-honoured traditions, looking to this duality to inspire their creativity and overall approach to gin making.

A contemporary gin, Adorn Beauty Gin is inspired by the botanicals found in luxury New Zealand skincare products including New Zealand flax seed, rose petals, organic rosehip, and chamomile.

1
of 400
BEAUTY GIN
ADORN
LIMITED

Hemp Gin

45% ABV

DISTILLERY: The National Distillery, Napier

VISIT THEM: 1 Ossian Street, Ahuriri, Napier

WEBSITE: nationaldistillery.nz

BOTANICALS: Juniper, Coriander Seed, Angelica Root, Manuka, Cardamom, Peppercorn, Almond, Liquorice Root, Hemp & Lemon Peel

---

TASTING NOTES: Savoury lemon freshness and aromatic spice on the nose. Dry palate with an earthy juniper presence emerging. Lingering spice and subtle lemon zest on the finish.

SERVING SUGGESTION: Enjoy with Fever-Tree Naturally-Light Indian Tonic Water and a sliver of lemon peel.

AWARDS: NZ Spirits Awards – Trophy Winner Best New Zealand Product in Category and Best Overall in Category 2020 & Gold 2020, San Francisco World Spirits Competition – Silver 2020, Ultimate Beverage Challenge USA – 89 Points 2020, Sip Awards – Bronze 2020 & Innovation Award 2020, and Australian Gin Awards Gold 2020

Ensconced in the commercial-industrial northern waterfront of Napier, The National Distillery Company resides in one of the cities architectural crown jewels. Built in 1931 following the Napier earthquake, it reflects the influences of Art Nouveau and Modernism, or Art Deco, that were in vogue at the time. They blend modern distilling techniques with time-honoured traditions, looking to this duality to inspire their creativity and overall approach to gin making.

A contemporary gin, Hemp Gin expands on their signature seven core gin aromatics by adding toasted hemp hearts and lashings of lemon peel.

AROMATIC BOTANICAL
HEMP GIN
HAND CRAFTED FROM TIME
HONOURED TRADITIONS
Abv – 45%   Vol – 750ml

NZ Native Gin - The Proof

44% ABV

DISTILLERY: The National Distillery, Napier

VISIT THEM: 1 Ossian Street, Ahuriri, Napier

WEBSITE: nationaldistillery.nz

BOTANICALS: Juniper, Coriander Seed, Angelica Root, Cardamom, Orris Root, Cassia Bark, Lemon Peel, Hemp, New Zealand Flax Seed, Kawakawa, Karamu & Liquorice Root

---

TASTING NOTES: Aromatic lemon freshness with cardamom and a hint of Kawakawa on the nose. Dry, earthy and herbaceous palate with juniper and subtle lemon on the finish.

SERVING SUGGESTION: Enjoy with Fever-Tree Refreshingly Light Indian Tonic Water and a slice of lemon.

AWARDS: The Junipers New Zealand Gin Awards – Gold Medal (Contemporary) 2020, Best in Class (Contemporary) 2020, Gold Medal (New Zealand Gin) 2020 & Best in Class (New Zealand Gin)

Ensconced in the commercial-industrial northern waterfront of Napier, The National Distillery Company resides in one of the cities architectural crown jewels. Built in 1931 following the Napier earthquake, it reflects the influences of Art Nouveau and Modernism, or Art Deco, that were in vogue at the time. They blend modern distilling techniques with time-honoured traditions, looking to this duality to inspire their creativity and overall approach to gin making.

A contemporary gin, NZ Native Gin - The Proof expands on their signature seven core gin aromatics by showcasing native kawakawa and karamu berries.

NZ NATIVE
GIN
THE PROOF
COPPER
DISTILLED
SPIRIT
NEW ZEALAND
AOTEAROA
HAND
CRAFTED
FROM TIME
HONOURED
TRADITIONS

1743 Riot

42% ABV

DISTILLERY: Riot & Rose Spirits, Blenheim
WEBSITE: riotandrose.com

BOTANICALS: Not Disclosed

TASTING NOTES: Bold notes of liquorice with distinctive citrus and herbal aromas. Dry palate with pleasant spice and earthy juniper, finishing clean with a subtle hint of citrus.

SERVING SUGGESTION: Enjoy with Fever-Tree Aromatic Tonic Water and a slice of orange.

AWARDS: Do Not Compete

Established in Blenheim at the heart of the Marlborough wine region, Riot & Rose is one of only a handful of distilleries in New Zealand that are female owned and operated. Forefronting this in their brand and ethos, they aim to create contemporary gins that allow you to reflect your own style. This is emphasised by the way that their gins are based on different time periods which were poignant in gin history.

A contemporary gin, 1743 Riot is a modern take on the traditional London Dry style paying homage to the London Gin Riots of 1743 and the bold, herbaceous flavours of that era.

NEW ZEALAND
RIOT & Rose
NEW WORLD GIN
42% Alc • Vol 700ml
R&R New World Gin • A modern, unique play on a timeless tipple from two distinct eras in two distinct gins.
RIOT
1743 REBELLION

1920 Rose

42% ABV

DISTILLERY: Riot & Rose Spirits, Blenheim
WEBSITE: riotandrose.com

BOTANICALS: Not Disclosed

TASTING NOTES: A highly aromatic nose, bursting with green manuka leaves and juniper. Balanced on the palate, fragrant undertones of cardamom and Indian spices with a long liquorice tail.

SERVING SUGGESTION: Enjoy with Fever-Tree Elderflower Tonic Water and a slice of cucumber.

AWARDS: Do Not Compete

Established in Blenheim at the heart of the Marlborough wine region, Riot & Rose is one of only a handful of distilleries in New Zealand that are female owned and operated. Forefronting this in their brand and ethos, they aim to create contemporary gins that allow you to reflect your own style. This is emphasised by the way that their gins are based on different time periods which were poignant in gin history.

A contemporary gin, 1920 Rose harks back to the romance and glamour of the Roaring Twenties and the flavours that saw gin come into vogue during that era including rose petal and cinnamon.

NEW ZEALAND
RIOT & Rose
NEW WORLD GIN
42% Alc • Vol 700ml
R&R New World Gin • A modern, unique play on a timeless tipple from two distinct eras in two distinct gins.
Rose
1920s Romance

Scapegrace Black

41.6% ABV

DISTILLERY: Scapegrace Distilling Co., Christchurch
WEBSITE: scapegracedistillery.com

BOTANICALS: Juniper, Aronia Berry, Sweet Potato, Butterfly Pea, Saffron, Pineapple & Others Not Disclosed

---

TASTING NOTES: Aromatic juniper with aronia berry and pineapple on the nose. Aronia berry and pineapple with hints of fresh citrus linger through to the finish with a subtle peppery spice emerging.

SERVING SUGGESTION: Enjoy with Fever-Tree Mediterranean Tonic Water and a slice of green apple.

Tucked away in the 'Garden City' of Christchurch, Scapegrace Distilling Co. makes their gin using glacial water that takes 80 years to filter through the rock of the Southern Alps before being released into an aquifer. They use a restored 19th century hand-beaten copper pot still to create their gins in the same way it was done back then. This is reflected in their bottles which are a modern take on the genever (Dutch gin) bottles from 200 years ago.

A contemporary gin, Scapegrace Black is the world's first black gin. Achieved through the use of aronia berry, saffron, pineapple, butterfly pea, and sweet potato, when paired with tonic its colour changes from black to purple.

BATCH N°
001
001
500
DISTILLED IN
NEW ZEALAND
N
SMALL PREMIUM BATCH
SCAPEGRACE
W E
BLACK GIN
NEW ZEALAND
BLACK
HANDCRAFTED
ARTISAN GIN
41.6% ABV
700ml

Totara Gin
40% ABV

DISTILLERY: Kiwi Spirit Distillery, Motupipi
VISIT THEM: 430 Abel Tasman Drive, Motupipi
WEBSITE: kiwispiritdistillery.co.nz

BOTANICALS: Not Disclosed

TASTING NOTES: Medicinal kahikatea and totara aroma. Dry, earthy palate with subtle juniper, kahikatea and totara lingering throughout and into the finish.

SERVING SUGGESTION: Enjoy with Fever-Tree Mediterranean Tonic Water and a slice of lemon.

AWARDS: Australia Gin Awards — Bronze 2019

Secluded in the beautiful Golden Bay area of the Tasman region, Totara take their name from the native New Zealand tree which is known for its traditional medicinal properties and fine timber. They use native New Zealand botanicals foraged from the local Tasman region's pristine native forests and water drawn from one of the aquifers that feeds the nearby Te Waikoropupū Springs, often considered the clearest spring water in the world.

A contemporary gin, Totara Gin is a fusion of old timey gin with native New Zealand botanicals and pure spring water.

HANDCRAFTED IN
NEW ZEALAND
TOTARA
GIN
NATIVE BOTANICALS, TWICE DISTILLED,
FUSED WITH THE PUREST WATER ON EARTH.
700ML   40% ALC/VOL

Victor Gin Kaffir Lime

42% ABV

DISTILLERY: Thomson Whisky Distillery, Riverhead

WEBSITE: thomsonwhisky.com

BOTANICALS: Juniper, Lemon, Lemongrass, Cardamom, Coriander Seed & Kaffir Lime

---

TASTING NOTES: Fragrant kaffir lime and lemongrass on the nose. A light body with bold kaffir lime and subtle cardamom spice on the palate, dry lingering finish with juniper emerging.

SERVING SUGGESTION: Enjoy with Fever-Tree Refreshingly Light Indian Tonic Water and a slice of lime.

AWARDS: NZ Spirits Awards – Silver 2020

Based in the historic township of Riverhead to the north of Auckland, Victor Gin was born out of tinkering and experimentation at the Thomson Whisky Distillery. Taking inspiration from the world of music they focus on fresh botanicals and the heavy use of juniper to create the best spirits they can.

A contemporary gin, Victor Gin Kaffir Lime expands on their Original gin's core flavours and concept with the single addition of kaffir lime in its botanicals.

VICTOR GIN
V
KAFFIR
LIME
NEW ZEALAND
42% ABV • 700 MLS

PINK & FLAVOURED

CONTAINING PINK, FLAVOURED, AND GIN LIQUEURS

Pink Gin – Gin traditionally flavoured with Angostura Bitters, the modern versions usually are flavoured with fruity profiles such as strawberries, raspberries and red currents.

Flavoured Gin – Distilled gins with one or more specifically noted and predominant botanicals other than juniper.

Gin Liqueur – Distilled gins that have been infused with additional flavourings and sweetened. The alcohol content will be lower, usually between 20-30% ABV.

___

batch10 Pink Gin
40% ABV

DISTILLERY: batch10 Spirits, Puhoi
WEBSITE: batch10.com

BOTANICALS: Juniper, Coriander Seed, Cassia Bark, Angelica Root, Nutmeg, Citrus Peel, Tangerine, Orris Root, Star Anise, Anise, Lemon, Orange, Cardamom, Pomegranate & Bitters

---

TASTING NOTES: Bold pomegranate and tangerine with smoked spice and a hint of cardamom on the nose. Juniper leads the palate with a burst of pomegranate and tangerine, earthy spice develops on the finish.

SERVING SUGGESTION: Enjoy with Fever-Tree Aromatic Tonic Water and pomegranate seeds.

Located in the idyllic backwoods of Puhoi, batch10 Spirits was started by a bunch of mates in one of their sheds infusing premium bourbon with local native bush honey. Having grown and developed since then they now make a range of distilled spirits crafted from the finest New Zealand and international ingredients.

A pink gin, batch10 Pink honours the historic recipe by balancing the light spice of bitters with the freshness of pomegranate in combination with their smooth London Dry Gin giving it a vibrant pink colour.

batch10
PINK
GIN

Blush Boysenberry Gin

37.5% ABV

WEBSITE: blushgin.co.nz

BOTANICALS: Boysenberry, Citrus Peel, Juniper, Anise, Cardamom & Angelica Root

---

TASTING NOTES: Bold fruity boysenberry with juniper and citrus on the nose. Emerging juniper on the palate with sweet boysenberry and a subtle citrus finish.

SERVING SUGGESTION: Enjoy with Fever-Tree Lemon Tonic Water and fresh boysenberries.

AWARDS: Australian Gin Awards – Silver 2019

Hidden amongst the urban sprawl of Auckland city, Blush was born from many experiments with all sorts of spirit infusions. Their vision is to change the perception of gin from that of "Mother's Ruin" to one of a lively and pleasant drink to be enjoyed. As natural products, it is important to store their gins in a cool dark place like a fine wine in order to retain their vibrant colours.

A flavoured gin, Blush Boysenberry is the world's first boysenberry gin, sourcing its star ingredient fresh from Nelson and imparting a bold dark red colour.

PRODUCED IN NEW ZEALAND
Nº 03
BLUSH
20   Small Batch   19
Boysenberry
GIN
37.5% ALC / Vol 70Cl
Triple Distilled | Hand Crafted | Batch Infused

Blush Rhubarb Gin

37.5% ABV

WEBSITE: blushgin.co.nz

BOTANICALS: Rhubarb, Juniper, Liquorice Root, Coriander Seed, Cassia Bark, Angelica Root, Nutmeg, Citrus Peel, Tangerine, Orris Root & Star Anise

---

TASTING NOTES: Aromatic spiced rhubarb with citrus and juniper undertones on the nose. Sweet rhubarb and berry fragrance on the palate with a touch of juniper, slight floral sweetness on the finish.

SERVING SUGGESTION: Enjoy with Fever-Tree Elderflower Tonic Water and a sprig of mint.

AWARDS: The Gin Is In Awards – Silver 2018

Hidden amongst the urban sprawl of Auckland city, Blush was born from many experiments with all sorts of spirit infusions. Their vision is to change the perception of gin from that of "Mother's Ruin" to one of a lively and pleasant drink to be enjoyed. As natural products, it is important to store their gins in a cool dark place like a fine wine in order to retain their vibrant colours.

A flavoured gin, the very first batch of Blush Rhubarb was actually made in a 500ml jam jar and has a deep pink colour.

PRODUCED IN NEW ZEALAND
Nº 01
BLUSH
Small Batch
Rhubarb
20   17
GIN
37.5% ALC / Vol 70Cl
Triple Distilled | Hand Crafted | Batch Infused

Blush Summer Citrus Gin
41.08% ABV

WEBSITE: blushgin.co.nz

BOTANICALS: Rhubarb, Juniper, Liquorice Root, Coriander Seed, Cassia Bark, Angelica Root, Nutmeg, Citrus Peel, Navel Orange, Lemon, Tangerine, Orris Root & Star Anise

---

TASTING NOTES: Sweet aromatic orange with a hint of lemon and rhubarb on the nose. Candied orange with lemon and subtle juniper on the palate, emerging rhubarb over a sweet finish.

SERVING SUGGESTION: Enjoy with Fever-Tree Lemon Tonic Water and a slice of orange.

Hidden amongst the urban sprawl of Auckland city, Blush was born from many experiments with all sorts of spirit infusions. Their vision is to change the perception of gin from that of "Mother's Ruin" to one of a lively and pleasant drink to be enjoyed. As natural products, it is important to store their gins in a cool dark place like a fine wine in order to retain their vibrant colours.

A flavoured gin, Blush Summer Citrus Gin is infused with citrus from sunny Kerikeri and rhubarb which give it a cloudy pale pink colour.

PRODUCED IN NEW ZEALAND
N° 05
BLUSH
Small Batch
Summer Citrus
GIN
20 20
41.08% ALC / Vol 70Cl
Triple Distilled | Hand Crafted | Batch Infused

Broken Heart Pinot Noir Gin

40% ABV

DISTILLERY: Broken Heart Spirits, Arrow Junction
VISIT THEM: 3 Whitechapel Road, Arrow Junction (by appointment)
WEBSITE: brokenheartspirits.com

BOTANICALS: Juniper, Coriander Seed, Lavender, Angelica Root & Others Not Disclosed

---

TASTING NOTES: Aromatic juniper with distinctive lavender and cherry on the nose. Creamy texture on the palate with bold juniper and subtle earth notes, sweet oriental spice and berry characters emerge on the finish.

SERVING SUGGESTION: Enjoy with Fever-Tree Lemon Tonic Water and a sprig of lavender.

AWARDS: NZ Spirits Awards — Silver 2020

Nestled in the foothills of the Southern Alps near picturesque Arrowtown, Broken Heart Spirits was born from the memory of a beloved life lost. They endeavour to create gin that captures the glory days of a friendship between two Germans that met in the South Island and bonded over their mutual appreciation for creating fine spirits before one of them tragically passed away.

A flavoured gin, Broken Heart Pinot Noir Gin cold-soaked in Central Otago pinot noir grapes, creating a soft and sweet spirit with an autumn red colour.

No 09
PINOT NOIR
GIN
BROKEN HEART
PINOT NOIR
GIN
No 09
No 09 Love Potion
BATCH No 001
40% ALC BY VOL.
500ML | NZ MADE
BOTTLE No 141 | 200

Broken Heart Quince Gin

30% ABV

DISTILLERY: Broken Heart Spirits, Arrow Junction
VISIT THEM: 3 Whitechapel Road, Arrow Junction (by appointment)
WEBSITE: brokenheartspirits.com

BOTANICALS: Juniper, Coriander Seed, Lavender, Angelica Root & Others Not Disclosed

---

TASTING NOTES: Bold quince with cinnamon-dusted apple pie aromas. Sweet quince with spiced fruit notes across the palate, emerging juniper on the finish.

SERVING SUGGESTION: Enjoy with Fever-Tree Refreshingly Light Indian Tonic Water and a cinnamon quill.

AWARDS: NZ Spirits Awards — Silver 2020

Nestled in the foothills of the Southern Alps near picturesque Arrowtown, Broken Heart Spirits was born from the memory of a beloved life lost. They endeavour to create gin that captures the glory days of a friendship between two Germans that met in the South Island and bonded over their mutual appreciation for creating fine spirits before one of them tragically passed away.

A flavoured gin, Broken Heart Quince Gin is cold-soaked in organic quince, a fruit often symbolically associated with love, and has a rich amber colour.

No 05
QUINCE
GIN
BROKEN HEART
QUINCE
GIN
No 05
No 05 Eternal Optimist
BATCH No. 001
30% ALC BY VOL.
500ML | NZ MADE
BOTTLE No 201 | 250

Broken Heart Rhubarb Gin

40% ABV

DISTILLERY: Broken Heart Spirits, Arrow Junction
VISIT THEM: 3 Whitechapel Road, Arrow Junction (by appointment)
WEBSITE: brokenheartspirits.com

BOTANICALS: Juniper, Coriander Seed, Lavender, Angelica Root, & Others Not Disclosed

---

TASTING NOTES: Distinctive sharp rhubarb with subtle hints of peppery lavender and juniper on the nose. Full rhubarb palate with a subtle tartness carrying on into the finish with hints of juniper emerging.

SERVING SUGGESTION: Enjoy with Fever-Tree Mediterranean Tonic Water and a slice of grapefruit.

Nestled in the foothills of the Southern Alps near picturesque Arrowtown, Broken Heart Spirits was born from the memory of a beloved life lost. They endeavour to create gin that captures the glory days of a friendship between two Germans that met in the South Island and bonded over their mutual appreciation for creating fine spirits before one of them tragically passed away.

A flavoured gin, Broken Heart Rhubarb Gin is infused with a combination of organic green, pink, and red rhubarb resulting in a peachy pink colour.

No 08
RHUBARB
GIN
BROKEN HEART
RHUBARB
GIN
No 08
No 08 Witchcraft
BATCH No 001
40% ALC BY VOL.
500ML | NZ MADE.
BOTTLE No 014 | 200

Black Doris Plum

38% ABV

DISTILLERY: Bureaucrats Gin Ltd., Wellington
WEBSITE: bureaucratsgin.co.nz

BOTANICALS: Juniper, Coriander Seed, Plum & Others Not Disclosed

---

TASTING NOTES: Bold cinnamon with a hint of plum on the nose. Mellow juniper on the palate with cinnamon and nutmeg lingering into the finish.

SERVING SUGGESTION: Enjoy with Fever-Tree Aromatic Tonic Water and a cinnamon quill.

AWARDS: NZ Spirits Awards – Bronze 2020

Located in the windy capital city of Wellington, Bureaucrats Gin Ltd.was started by two bureaucrats with the hobby of distilling gin in their home laundries. Driven by a love of fine gin and fine things they used the age old method of trial and error until they had developed a distillation consistency and quality which they could share with the world. Producing small batches, they focus on innovation and bold botanical combinations.

A flavoured gin, Black Doris Plum includes a combination of black doris plums and spices resulting in a delicate purple hue.

BUREAUCRATS GIN
THE BUREAUCRATS
BLACK DORIS PLUM
WELLINGTON
GIN
DISTILLED AND BOTTLED BY HAND
Batch no: 0026
70CL
BUREAUCRATS
GIN LTD
38% ALC. VOL.

Curiosity Gin - Pinot Barrel Sloe

27% ABV

DISTILLERY: The Spirits Workshop Distillery, Christchurch
VISIT THEM: 11 Sandyford Street, Sydenham, Christchurch
WEBSITE: thespiritsworkshop.co.nz

BOTANICALS: Juniper, Manuka Berries & Leaves, Coriander Seed, Cardamom, Orange Zest, Angelica Root, Lavender, Cinnamon, Star Anise & Sloe Berries

---

TASTING NOTES: Deeply sweet with Christmas cake spice that carries on deep into the palate, subtle almond and sweet plum develop over the finish.

SERVING SUGGESTION: Enjoy with Fever-Tree Lemon Tonic Water and a slice of lemon.

AWARDS: NZ Spirits Awards — Silver 2020

Established in the light industrial area of Christchurch's suburb Sydenham, Curiosity Gin set out from the start to create truly unique and individual gins that stand out from the crowd and the tonic. To hold true to these values their gins are made "grain to glass" where possible, in small batches using their copper pot still.

A sloe gin, Curiosity Gin Pinot Barrel Sloe is a gin liqueur made the traditional way by steeping sloe berries in their Curious Dry Gin in barrels previously used to age Otago Pinot Noir for several months.

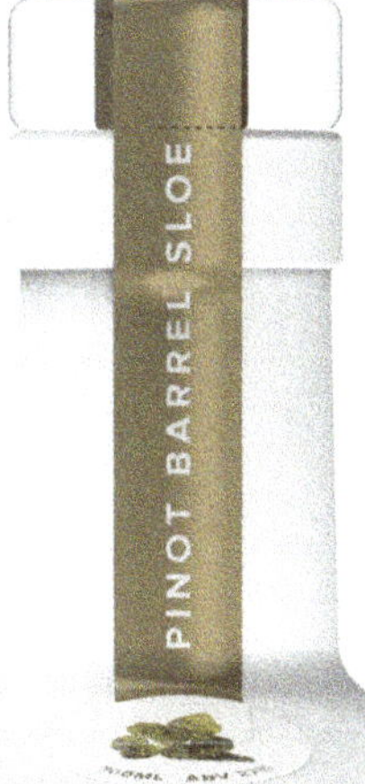
PINOT BARREL SLOE

CURIOSITY GIN
GIN
CURIOSITY

Curiosity Gin — Ruby

37.5% ABV

DISTILLERY: The Spirits Workshop Distillery, Christchurch
VISIT THEM: 11 Sandyford Street, Sydenham, Christchurch
WEBSITE: thespiritsworkshop.co.nz

BOTANICALS: Juniper, Tarata, Kawakawa, Horopito, Manuka & Rhubarb

---

TASTING NOTES: Honey and floral rhubarb aroma on the nose. Very sweet palate with an emerging herbaceous lemon on the finish.

SERVING SUGGESTION: Enjoy with Fever-Tree Lemon Tonic Water and a slice of lemon.

AWARDS: NZ Spirits Awards — Silver 2020

Established in the light industrial area of Christchurch's suburb Sydenham, Curiosity Gin set out from the start to create truly unique and individual gins that stand out from the crowd and the tonic. To hold true to these values their gins are made "grain to glass" where possible, in small batches using their copper pot still.

A flavoured gin, Curiosity Gin Ruby is made by infusing their Curiosity Dry Gin with fresh Otaki rhubarb stalks and a little added sweetness resulting in a delicate cloudy red.

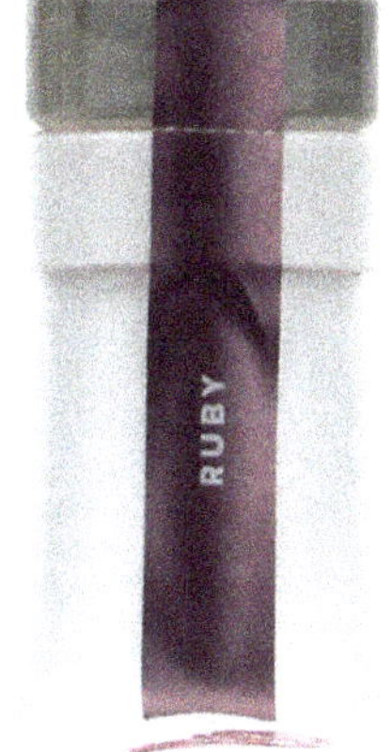

RUBY

CURIOSITY GIN
GIN
CURIOSITY

Dancing Sands Chocolate Gin

44% ABV

DISTILLERY: Dancing Sands Distillery, Takaka

VISIT THEM: 46A Commercial Street, Takaka

WEBSITE: dancingsands.com

BOTANICALS: Juniper, Coriander Seed, Angelica Root, Manuka, Cardamom, Peppercorn, Almond, Liquorice Root, Cocoa & Red Bush Tea Leaves

---

TASTING NOTES: Bitter chocolate aroma with cardamom and nutmeg spice. Peppery palate with hints of juniper, ginger and cacao, dry finish with lingering bitter chocolate.

SERVING SUGGESTION: Enjoy with Fever-Tree Ginger Ale and a slice of orange.

AWARDS: NZ Spirits Awards – Bronze 2019

Bundled away in the small town of Takaka in the Tasman region's beautiful Golden Bay area, Dancing Sands Distillery sources their water from the aquifer that feeds the nearby Te Waikoropupū Springs, often regarded as the clearest spring water in the world. They make all of their gins in small 150 litre batches to allow for maximum control over quality without any automation, instead using taste, temperature, and touch to achieve their results.

A flavoured gin, Dancing Sands Chocolate Gin is New Zealand's first collaboration gin, partnering with cocktail institution C.G.R. Merchant and Co. with a rich brown colour.

DANCING SANDS
CHOCOLATE GIN
44% ABV
700ML
HANDCRAFTED & MADE IN
NEW ZEALAND
THE
SPIRIT
OF
COLLABORATION
C.G.R. Merchant & Co.

Dancing Sands Saffron Gin

46% ABV

DISTILLERY: Dancing Sands Distillery, Takaka

VISIT THEM: 46A Commercial Street, Takaka

WEBSITE: dancingsands.com

BOTANICALS: Juniper, Coriander Seed, Angelica Root, Manuka, Cardamom, Peppercorn, Almond, Liquorice Root, Saffron & Rosebud

---

TASTING NOTES: Earthy root notes with cardamom spice and a suggestion of saffron on the nose. Dry palate with cardamom spice and peppery juniper, subtle saffron and honey sweetness emerge on the finish.

SERVING SUGGESTION: Enjoy with Fever-Tree Refreshingly Light Tonic Water and a slice of orange.

AWARDS: Sip Awards – Gold 2018, NZ Spirits Awards – Bronze 2019, and San Francisco World Spirit Awards – Gold Medal 2018 & Silver Medal 2019

Bundled away in the small town of Takaka in the Tasman region's beautiful Golden Bay area, Dancing Sands Distillery sources their water from the aquifer that feeds the nearby Te Waikoropupū Springs, often regarded as the clearest spring water in the world. They make all of their gins in small 150 litre batches to allow for maximum control over quality without any automation, instead using taste, temperature, and touch to achieve their results.

A flavoured gin, it takes over 8,000 hand-picked crocus flowers to make a single batch of Dancing Sands Saffron Gin resulting in a pale yellow colour.

DANCING SANDS
SAFFRON GIN
46% ABV
700ML
HANDCRAFTED & MADE IN
NEW ZEALAND

Dancing Sands Sun-Kissed Gin

37.5% ABV

DISTILLERY: Dancing Sands Distillery, Takaka

VISIT THEM: 46A Commercial Street, Takaka

WEBSITE: dancingsands.com

BOTANICALS: Juniper, Coriander Seed, Angelica Root, Manuka, Cardamom, Peppercorn, Almond, Liquorice Root, Strawberry & Rhubarb

---

TASTING NOTES: Creamy almond, spiced rhubarb and a hint of strawberry on the nose. Sweet strawberry and rhubarb with a creamy vanilla palate, subtle almond and liquorice emerging on the finish.

SERVING SUGGESTION: Enjoy with Fever-Tree Lemon Tonic Water and fresh strawberries.

AWARDS: Sip Awards – Silver 2019, NZ Spirits Awards – Silver 2019, and San Francisco World Spirit Awards – Bronze Medal 2019

Bundled away in the small town of Takaka in the Tasman region's beautiful Golden Bay area, Dancing Sands Distillery sources their water from the aquifer that feeds the nearby Te Waikoropupū Springs, often regarded as the clearest spring water in the world. They make all of their gins in small 150 litre batches to allow for maximum control over quality without any automation, instead using taste, temperature, and touch to achieve their results.

A flavoured gin, Dancing Sands Sun-Kissed Gin is made using fresh strawberries and locally sourced rhubarb which are then candied before infusion giving it a pale pink colour.

DANCING SANDS
••• SUN-KISSED GIN •••
STRAWBERRY & RHUBARB
HANDCRAFTED & MADE
IN NEW ZEALAND
37.5 ABV
700ML

Day Off Feijoa Gin
45% ABV

DISTILLERY: Good George Distillery, Hamilton
WEBSITE: goodgeorge.co.nz

BOTANICALS: Juniper, Coriander Seed, Angelica Root, Rosehip, Liquorice Root, Pink Peppercorn, Feijoa, Cardamom, Lime & Star Anise

---

TASTING NOTES: Fragrant feijoa aroma with hints of vanilla, liquorice and cinnamon on the nose. Bold peppery feijoa on the palate with subtle lime and honey notes, dry finish with lingering spice.

SERVING SUGGESTION: Enjoy with Fever-Tree Refreshingly Light Indian Tonic Water and a fresh feijoa.

AWARDS: NZ Spirits Awards – Silver 2020 and London Spirits Competition – Bronze 2020

Cloistered in the industrial suburb of Frankton in Hamilton, Good George Distillery resides in the former St George's Church from which they take their name. Originally started as a brewery, they also began making hand sanitiser in early 2020 as part of Operation Helping Hands and later decided to give their stills a day off from that project and make some gin too.

A flavoured gin, Day Off Feijoa Gin draws on their experience of adding a feijoa spin to their other products by adding 40kg of them to the still after distillation.

BOTTLE NO.
001
SMALL BATCH DISTILLED IN
GOOD George DISTILLING
THE OLD SAINT GEORGE CHURCH
16
17
DAY OFF
SMALL Feijoa BATCH
750 ML
GIN
45% ABV
HAND CRAFTED IN NEW ZEALAND

Damson Plum & Blackberry Gin Liqueur

32% ABV

DISTILLERY: imagination, Reikorangi

WEBSITE: imaginationgin.nz

BOTANICALS: Juniper, Corriander Seed, Cinnamon, Liquorice Root, Orris Root, Orange, Lime, Lemon, Manuka, Damon Plums & Blackberries

---

TASTING NOTES: Sweet plum and subtle fresh lemon aroma. Very sweet palate with dominant plum, a subtle hint of lemon and spice on the finish.

SERVING SUGGESTION: Enjoy with Fever-Tree Lemon Tonic Water and a slice of lemon.

AWARDS: NZ Spirits Awards – Bronze 2020

Sheltered in the lush foothills of the Reikorangi Valley on the Kapiti Coast, imagination is housed on the original site of the pioneering Tuatara Beer Brewery which they use to draw inspiration from. They produce small batch seasonal gins using a copper plate fractionating column still and pure rainwater captured on the property, and source many of their ingredients locally from family owned operations and backyard gardeners.

A gin liqueur, Damson Plum & Blackberry Gin Liqueur is inspired by an old English recipe that highlights New Zealand's seasonal autumn produce including plums that were macerated in their dry gin for four months giving it a deep purple red colour.

your imagination should be used
imagination
DAMSON PLUM
& BLACKBERRY
NEW ZEALAND GIN LIQUEUR
ABV 32% | 700ml

Reikorangi Rhubarb and Raspberry Gin

38% ABV

DISTILLERY: imagination, Reikorangi

WEBSITE: imaginationgin.nz

BOTANICALS: Juniper, Coriander Seed, Angelica Root, Manuka, Cardamom, Peppercorn, Almond & Liquorice Root

---

TASTING NOTES: Perfumed cinnamon with bold raspberry and a hint of sweet liquorice aroma. A full palate of rhubarb, raspberry, and cinnamon that lingers into the peppery citrus finish.

SERVING SUGGESTION: Enjoy with Fever-Tree Aromatic Tonic Water and fresh raspberries.

AWARDS: NZ Spirits Awards – Silver 2020

Sheltered in the lush foothills of the Reikorangi Valley on the Kapiti Coast, imagination is housed on the original site of the pioneering Tuatara Beer Brewery which they use to draw inspiration from. They produce small batch seasonal gins using a copper plate fractionating column still and pure rainwater captured on the property, and source many of their ingredients locally from family owned operations and backyard gardeners.

A flavoured gin, Reikorangi Rhubarb and Raspberry Gin is inspired by the New Zealand summer using raspberries macerated in a floral dry gin and blended with slowly extracted rhubarb juice which gives it a bold pink red colour.

laughter is timeless, imagination has
imagination
RHUBARB
AND
RASPBERRY
REIKORANGI
RHUBARB & RASPBERRY
NEW ZEALAND GIN
ABV 38% | 700ml

Lavender Infused Gin

40% ABV

DISTILLERY: Lavender Hill, Riverhead

VISIT THEM: 11 Beacon Road, Riverhead

WEBSITE: lavenderhill.co.nz

BOTANICALS: Juniper, Coriander Seed, Cassia Bark, Angelica Root, Nutmeg, Citrus Peel, Tangerine, Orris Root, Star Anise, Anise, Lemon, Orange, Cardamom & Lavandula Angustifolia

---

TASTING NOTES: Light floral lavender with hints of spice and fresh citrus on the nose. Dry palate with bold juniper and spicy bitterness, lingering peppery finish with a hint of citrus peel.

SERVING SUGGESTION: Enjoy with Fever-Tree Elderflower Tonic Water and a slice of lemon.

AWARDS: NZ Spirits Awards – Silver 2020

Secluded on the outskirts of the historic township of Riverhead to the north of Auckland, Lavender Hill operates from a small working farm. Their central philosophy is to create products with a connection to the land and superb provenance, using handcrafted and sustainable ingredients to achieve this.

A flavoured gin, Lavender Infused Gin is made using the essential oils from their own commercial fields of 'Pacific Blue' English lavender (Angustifolia) which is hand harvested and extracted on the farm.

LAVENDER HILL

TRIPLE DISTILLED

Lavender INFUSED **GIN**

MADE WITH
100% PURE
LAVANDULA ANGUSTIFOLIA
BLENDED WITH 14 BOTANICALS

FIELD

#2

HANDCRAFTED.
INFUSED WITH OUR
OWN PURE LAVENDER
OIL FROM FIELD#2

40% Alc by Vol
80 Proof

700ml
22 Std Drinks

PRODUCED BY
LAVENDER HILL FARM
PRODUCT OF NEW ZEALAND

#lavenderhillnz
lavenderhill.co.nz

Saffron Infused Gin

40% ABV

DISTILLERY: Lavender Hill, Riverhead
VISIT THEM: 11 Beacon Road, Riverhead
WEBSITE: lavenderhill.co.nz

BOTANICALS: Juniper, Coriander Seed, Cassia Bark, Angelica Root, Nutmeg, Citrus Peel, Tangerine, Orris Root, Star Anise, Anise, Lemon, Orange, Cardamom & Saffron

---

TASTING NOTES: Mellow citrus peel and subtle saffron on the nose. Toasted coriander freshness and a hint of saffron on the palate that lingers through to the finish with a subtle honey sweetness.

SERVING SUGGESTION: Enjoy with Fever-Tree Refreshingly Light Tonic Water and a slice of orange.

AWARDS: NZ Spirits Awards – Bronze 2020

Secluded on the outskirts of the historic township of Riverhead to the north of Auckland, Lavender Hill operates from a small working farm. Their central philosophy is to create products with a connection to the land and superb provenance, using handcrafted and sustainable ingredients to achieve this.

A flavoured gin, Saffron Infused Gin is made using 100% organic saffron from a partner farm in the South Island producing a vibrant yellow colour.

WINE ORBIT
93+/100
wineorbit.co.nz

AWARDED
SILVER
New Zealand
Spirits Awards

LAVENDER HILL
TRIPLE DISTILLED
Saffron
INFUSED
GIN

AKL

MADE WITH
100% PURE
ORGANIC SAFFRON
BLENDED WITH 14 BOTANICALS

MADE WITH THE PURE
STIGMA OR "THREADS"
FROM THE CROCUS SATIVUS
(SAFFRON FLOWER). GROWN
AND HAND HARVESTED IN
SUNNY NELSON, NZ.

40% Alc by Vol
80 Proof

700ml
22 Std Drinks

PRODUCED BY
LAVENDER HILL FARM
PRODUCT OF NEW ZEALAND

#lavenderhillnz
lavenderhill.co.nz

Little Biddy Gin - Pink
43% ABV

DISTILLERY: Reefton Distilling Co., Reefton
VISIT THEM: 10 Smith Street, Reefton
WEBSITE: reeftondistillingco.com

BOTANICALS: Tayberries, Lavender, Blueberries, Navel Oranges, Rosemary, Kanuka, Tarata, Angelica, Cardamon, Cassia, Corriander Seed, Liquorice Root, Juniper & Orris Root

---

TASTING NOTES: Bold berry with subtle cardamom on the nose. Cardamom spice and herbal notes emerge on the palate, finishing with subtle peppery juniper and floral berry sweetness.

SERVING SUGGESTION: Enjoy with Fever-Tree Mediterranean Tonic Water and fresh raspberries.

Stationed deep in the Inangahua River Valley in the West Coast town of Reefton, Little Biddy is named in honour of the local legend Bridget 'Biddy' Goodwin, a pipe-smoking, gin-toting, 4-foot-tall gold prospector who lived in the 1800s. A modern distillery in an age-old town, Reefton Distilling Co. use large numbers of native botanicals from the surrounding rainforest to achieve a distinct West Coast flavour.

A pink gin, Little Biddy Gin – Pink is made with hand-picked, locally grown spray-free berries resulting in a deep rich pink colour.

BATCH Nº
20/001
SMALL BATCH
DISTILLED
LITTLE BIDDY
New Zealand Botanical Gin
PINK
Tayberries + Lavender
+ Blueberries + Navel Oranges
+ Rosemary + Kanuka + Tarata +
Angelica + Cardamom + Cassia
+ Coriander + Liquorice +
Juniper + Orris Root
43% ABV | 700ml
Handcrafted + Small Batch Distilled + Bottled in Reefton, West Coast, New Zealand

Adorn Rosé Beauty Gin
42% ABV

DISTILLERY: The National Distillery Company, Napier
VISIT THEM: 1 Ossian Street, Ahuriri, Napier
WEBSITE: nationaldistillery.nz

BOTANICALS: Juniper, Coriander Seed, Angelica Root, Cardamom, Orris Root, Cassia Bark, Lemon Peel, Rosehip, Rose Petals, Chamomile, New Zealand Flax Seed & Liquorice Root

---

TASTING NOTES: Floral rose and lemon peel aroma with lifted juniper on the nose. Juniper, chamomile and rose notes emerge on the palate with hints of cardamom and a light lemon coriander freshness on the finish.

SERVING SUGGESTION: Enjoy with Fever-Tree Elderflower Tonic Water and a slice of lemon.

Ensconced in the commercial-industrial northern waterfront of Napier, The National Distillery Company resides in one of the cities architectural crown jewels. Built in 1931 following the Napier earthquake, it reflects the influences of Art Nouveau and Modernism, or Art Deco, that were in vogue at the time. They blend modern distilling techniques with time-honoured traditions, looking to this duality to inspire their creativity and overall approach to gin making.

A flavoured gin, Adorn Rosé Beauty Gin is inspired by the botanicals found in luxury New Zealand skincare products with a focus on rose petals and organic rosehip, giving it a bold dark red colour.

of 400
BEAUTY GIN
ADORN
ROSÉ

Solace Cranberry & Raspberry Gin

37.5% ABV

DISTILLERY: Kings Liquor, Auckland
WEBSITE: solacegin.co.nz

BOTANICALS: Juniper, Coriander Seed, Cassia Bark, Angelica Root, Nutmeg, Citrus Peel, Tangerine, Orris Root, Star Anise, Anise, Lemon, Orange, Cardamom & Natural Berry Extract

---

TASTING NOTES: Aromatic juniper and cranberry on the nose. Juniper and cranberry notes carry throughout the palate and linger into the finish with a hint of citrus emerging.

SERVING SUGGESTION: Enjoy with Fever-Tree Refreshingly Light Indian Tonic Water and fresh raspberries.

Huddled on the northern edge of Auckland in the suburb of Rosedale, Solace Gin is produced by Kings Liquor which has been producing spirits since 1985. They produce small, handcrafted, artisanal batches of triple distilled gin which is echoed in their hand-illustrated labels that reflect the traditional crafting and blending of their recipes.

A flavoured gin, Solace Cranberry & Raspberry Gin uses their Dry Gin as a base and is then sweetened with natural berry extracts which also give it a deep pink colour.

HAND CRAFTED
SOLACE
GIN
PREMIUM
TRIPLE DISTILLED
Cranberry & Raspberry
KIN
EST.
EXPERTLY
Small Batch gently infused
WITH SELECT BOTANICALS
CRAFTED
700ML
BOTTLED IN NEW ZEALAND
37.5% ALC VOL

WHITE SHEEP <u>CO</u>

New Zealand

Sheep Milk & Honey Gin

42% ABV

DISTILLERY: The White Sheep Co., Whangamata
WEBSITE: thewhitesheepco.com

BOTANICALS: Juniper, Manuka Honey, Angelica Root, Orris Root, Clementine Zest, Coriander Seed, Lemon Zest & Allspice

---

TASTING NOTES: Creamy vanilla with hints of sweet honey on the nose. Light juniper and subtly sweet vanilla across the palate, emerging honeyed spice notes on the finish.

SERVING SUGGESTION: Enjoy neat or with Fever-Tree Refreshingly Light Tonic Water.

AWARDS: New Zealand Food Awards – Best Alcoholic Beverage 2019 Innovation Award 2019, NZ Spirits Awards– Bronze 2020 and CWSA – Gold Medal 2020

Located in the popular beach town of Whangamata which borders The Coromandel Forest Park, The White Sheep Co. is a boutique distillery that handcrafts a range of spirits and liqueurs using premium New Zealand sheep's milk. The milk takes two weeks to ferment using special yeasts and is then distilled into a full strength spirit using a traditional style copper still to retain some of the sheep milk's flavours.

A flavoured gin, Sheep Milk & Honey Gin includes premium local honey among its botanicals which evokes the idea of New Zealand being a 'land of milk and honey' and imparts a golden hue.

WHITE SHEEP Co
SHEEP MILK & HONEY GIN
New Zealand

Wild Diamond Feijoa Gin

42% ABV

DISTILLERY: Wild Diamond Distillery, Wanaka

WEBSITE: wilddiamond.co.nz

BOTANICALS: Juniper, Coriander Seed, Angelica Root, Cassia, Liquorice Extract, Cinnamon, Almond, Feijoa & Others Not Disclosed

---

TASTING NOTES: Sweet vanilla and dominating almond with a hint of feijoa on the nose. Juniper and cinnamon emerge on the palate with a dry spicy finish.

SERVING SUGGESTION: Enjoy with Fever-Tree Mediterranean Tonic Water and a fresh feijoa.

Sheltered between the foothills of the Southern Alps and Lake Wanaka, Wild Diamond Distillery takes its name from the natural elements that surround them. They select their botanicals based on their quality and character, sourcing them both internationally and locally. Maintaining their connection to their environment, their stills are powered by renewable wind and water energy, and they invest back into water and aquatic habitat enhancement, recovery, and restoration initiatives.

A flavoured gin, Wild Diamond Feijoa Gin is a limited edition that uses their Rare Dry Gin as the base with an extra infusion of organic feijoa giving it a soft golden colour.

WILD DIAMOND
Feijoa Gin
~ Limited Edition ~
Distiller:

Wild Diamond Vanilla Gin

42% ABV

DISTILLERY: Wild Diamond Distillery, Wanaka

WEBSITE: wilddiamond.co.nz

BOTANICALS: Juniper, Coriander Seed, Angelica Root, Cassia, Liquorice Extract, Cinnamon, Almond, Vanilla & Others Not Disclosed

---

TASTING NOTES: Aromatic juniper with vanilla, almond, and root spice on the nose. Dry palate with juniper, earthy spice, and a touch of bitter almond, juniper lingers with a very subtle hint of vanilla on the finish.

SERVING SUGGESTION: Enjoy with Fever-Tree Refreshingly Light Indian Tonic Water.

Sheltered between the foothills of the Southern Alps and Lake Wanaka, Wild Diamond Distillery takes its name from the natural elements that surround them. They select their botanicals based on their quality and character, sourcing them both internationally and locally. Maintaining their connection to their environment, their stills are powered by renewable wind and water energy, and they invest back into water and aquatic habitat enhancement, recovery, and restoration initiatives.

A flavoured gin, Wild Diamond Vanilla Gin is a limited edition that uses their Rare Dry Gin as the base with an extra infusion of organic vanilla giving it a pale golden colour.

WILD DIAMOND
Vanilla Gin
- Limited Edition -
Distiller:

Wild Diamond Saffron Gin

41.6% ABV

DISTILLERY: Wild Diamond Distillery, Wanaka

WEBSITE: wilddiamond.co.nz

BOTANICALS: Juniper, Coriander Seed, Angelica Root, Cassia, Liquorice Extract, Cinnamon, Almond, Saffron & 19 Others Not Disclosed

---

TASTING NOTES: Aromatic earthy root notes with saffron and lime on the nose. Juniper and spice lead the palate with subtle saffron and honey into the finish.

SERVING SUGGESTION: Enjoy with Fever-Tree Refreshingly Light Tonic Water.

Sheltered between the foothills of the Southern Alps and Lake Wanaka, Wild Diamond Distillery takes its name from the natural elements that surround them. They select their botanicals based on their quality and character, sourcing them both internationally and locally. Maintaining their connection to their environment, their stills are powered by renewable wind and water energy, and they invest back into water and aquatic habitat enhancement, recovery, and restoration initiatives.

A flavoured gin, Wild Diamond Saffron Gin is a limited edition that uses their Rare Dry Gin as the base with an extra infusion of saffron giving it a bright yellow colour.

WILD DIAMOND
Saffron Gin
- Limited Edition -
Distiller:

1919 Pineapple Bits Gin
41% ABV

DISTILLERY: 1919 Distilling, Auckland
WEBSITE: 1919distilling.com

BOTANICALS: Juniper, Coriander Seed, Lemon Peel, Orange Peel, Angelica Root, Pineapple & Cacao Nibs

---

TASTING NOTES: Distinctive sweet pineapple with juicy citrus aromas. Creamy texture with sweet pineapple and orange on the palate, lingering sweet finish with citrus undertones.

SERVING SUGGESTION: Enjoy with Fever-Tree Refreshingly Light Indian Tonic Water and a slice of pineapple.

AWARDS: The Junipers New Zealand Gin Awards – Gold 2020

Nestled in the bustling industrial area of East Tamaki, 1919 Distilling prides itself on sourcing everything locally, even down to their custom made still, so that they can ensure the best quality and craftsmanship. Named for the year that New Zealand voted down prohibition they also stay true to the way gin was made in the 1900's by using ethanol made from cane sugar rather than whey.

A distinct flavoured gin, 1919 Pineapple Bits Gin is all about classic Kiwiana with its taste of pineapple and chocolate and pale yellow colour.

NZ MADE
1919
DISTILLING
PINEAPPLE BITS
GIN
Est. 2017
HAND-CRAFTED
SMALL BATCH
700ml
NEW ZEALAND MADE, DISTILLED & BOTTLED
ALC BY VOL 41%
82 PROOF

1919 Pink Gin

41% ABV

DISTILLERY: 1919 Distilling, Auckland
WEBSITE: 1919distilling.com

BOTANICALS: Juniper, Coriander Seed, Green Cardamom, Lemon Peel, Orange Peel, Angelica Root, Cherries, Manuka Honey, Cinnamon, Strawberries & Raspberries

---

TASTING NOTES: Bold aromatic juniper with hints of citrus, spice and strawberry on the nose. A very clean, dry palate with lifted juniper and spice, subtle honey and strawberry sweetness for a long, balanced lingering finish.

SERVING SUGGESTION: Enjoy with Fever-Tree Lemon Tonic Water and fresh strawberries.

AWARDS: New Zealand Artisan Awards – Alcohol Category Winner 2019, New Zealand Spirits Award – Bronze 2020 and Sip Awards – Platinum 2020 & Innovation Award 2020

Nestled in the bustling industrial area of East Tamaki, 1919 Distilling prides itself on sourcing everything locally, even down to their custom made still, so that they can ensure the best quality and craftsmanship. Named for the year that New Zealand voted down prohibition they also stay true to the way gin was made in the 1900's by using ethanol made from cane sugar rather than whey.

A pink gin, the 1919 Pink Gin is distilled using raspberries and 100% Auckland grown strawberries to capture the taste of summer and impart a pale pink colour.

GUIDE TO NEW ZEALAND GIN
— 2020 —
TASTERS'
PICK

100% NZ MADE
DISTILLING
1919
GIN
Est. 2017
HAND-CRAFTED
SMALL BATCH
700ml
100% NEW ZEALAND MADE, DISTILLED & BOTTLED
ALC BY VOL 41%
82 PROOF

BARREL AGED

CONTAINING BARREL AGED GINS

Barrel Aged Gin – Gins that have been aged post – distillation in any wooden barrel for a chosen length of time.

____

Broken Heart Barrel Aged Gin

40% ABV

DISTILLERY: Broken Heart Spirits, Arrow Junction

VISIT THEM: 3 Whitechapel Road, Arrow Junction (by appointment)

WEBSITE: brokenheartspirits.com

BOTANICALS: Juniper, Coriander Seed, Lavender, Angelica
& Others Not Disclosed

AGING PROCESS: Aged six months in a French Chardonnay Barrel.

TASTING NOTES: Fragrant lavender with an oaky vanilla complexity on the nose. Juniper leads the palate with subtle notes of honey and vanilla, creamy toasted oak on the finish.

SERVING SUGGESTION: Enjoy neat or with Fever-Tree Soda Water.

Nestled in the foothills of the Southern Alps near picturesque Arrowtown, Broken Heart Spirits was born from the memory of a beloved life lost. They endeavour to create gin that captures the glory days of a friendship between two Germans that met in the South Island and bonded over their mutual appreciation for creating fine spirits before one of them tragically passed away.

A barrel aged gin that spends a year in French chardonnay oak, Broken Heart Barrel Aged Gin is warm and welcoming with a delicate golden hue.

Nº 04
BARREL AGED
GIN
BROKEN HEART
BARREL AGED
GIN
Nº 04
Nº 04   Time Heals
BATCH Nº 001
40% ALC BY VOL.   500ML. | NZ MADE
BOTTLE Nº 120 | 450

Curiosity Gin - Negroni Special

55% ABV

DISTILLERY: The Spirits Workshop Distillery, Christchurch
VISIT THEM: 11 Sandyford Street, Sydenham, Christchurch
WEBSITE: thespiritsworkshop.co.nz

BOTANICALS: Juniper, Coriander Seed, Orange Zest, Lime Zest, Ginger Root, Angelica Root, Lavender, Cinnamon, Cardamom & Star Anise

---

AGING PROCESS: Aged in new French Oak Barrels for 6-8 weeks.

TASTING NOTES: Bold aromatic juniper, orange cinnamon and spicy cardamom on the nose. Bold and dry with a subtle honey sweetness and floral spice on the palate, aromatic juniper develops over the finish with fresh lemon zest.

SERVING SUGGESTION: Enjoy with Fever-Tree Aromatic Tonic Water and a slice of orange.

AWARDS: New York World Wine and Spirits Competition — Silver 2017, San Francisco World Spirits Competition Gold 2018, SIPS Awards — Silver 2018, and NZ Spirits Awards — Silver 2019 & Gold 2020

Established in the light industrial area of Christchurch's suburb Sydenham, Curiosity Gin set out from the start to create truly unique and individual gins that stand out from the crowd and the tonic. To hold true to these values their gins are made "grain to glass" where possible, in small batches using their copper pot still.

A barrel aged gin, Curiosity Negroni Special is rested in new French Oak barrels and designed to complement a Negroni cocktail with a soft golden hue.

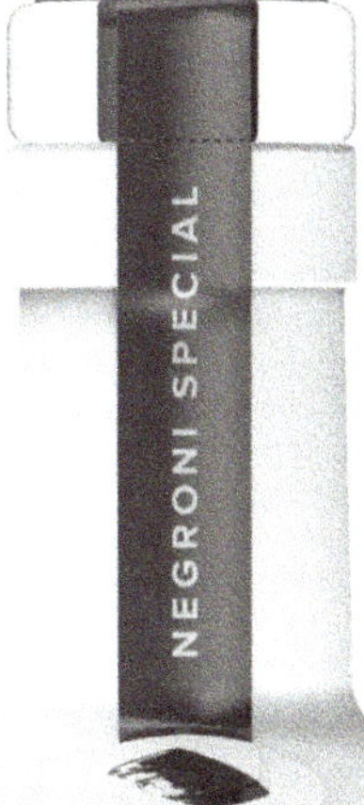
NEGRONI SPECIAL
CURIOSITY GIN
GIN
CURIOSITY

Dancing Sands Barrel Aged Gin

48% ABV

DISTILLERY: Dancing Sands Distillery, Takaka

VISIT THEM: 46A Commercial Street, Takaka

WEBSITE: dancingsands.com

BOTANICALS: Juniper, Coriander Seed, Angelica Root, Manuka, Cardamom, Peppercorn, Almond & Liquorice Root

---

AGING PROCESS: Aged 3 Months in 14 Year Golden Rum Cask and French Oak Barrels.

TASTING NOTES: Bold aromatic juniper with spicy cardamom and a hint of liquorice rum sweetness on the nose. A full palate of juniper with honeyed almond notes and a burst of spice, pepper and sweet liquorice notes emerge on the finish.

SERVING SUGGESTION: Enjoy neat or with Fever-Tree Soda Water.

AWARDS: Sip Awards – Platinum 2018 & 19, The Gin Masters – 2017 Gold & 2018 Silver, NZ Spirits Awards – Silver 2019 & Gold 2020, and San Francisco World Spirit Awards – Silver Medal 2017 & 19

Bundled away in the small town of Takaka in the Tasman region's beautiful Golden Bay area, Dancing Sands Distillery sources their water from the aquifer that feeds the nearby Te Waikoropupū Springs, often regarded as the clearest spring water in the world. They make all of their gins in small 150 litre batches to allow for maximum control over quality without any automation, instead using taste, temperature, and touch to achieve their results.

A barrel aged gin that spends three months in both new French oak barrels and 14-year old Murderer's Bay Gold Rum barrels, Dancing Sands Barrel Aged Gin has a soft golden colour.

DANCING SANDS
BARREL AGED GIN
48% ABV
700ML
HANDCRAFTED & MADE IN
NEW ZEALAND

The Pioneer
46% ABV

DISTILLERY: Fenton Street Distillery, Taranaki
VISIT THEM: 11 Fenton St, Stratford (by appointment)
WEBSITE: fentonartscollective.co.nz/distillery

BOTANICALS: Juniper, Coriander Seed, Cassia Bark, Ginger, Kawakawa, Tarata, Angelica, Lemon Zest, Horopito, Pepper, Bush Honey, Manuka & Nutmeg

---

TASTING NOTES: Aromatically complex with bold cinnamon and Christmas spice on the nose and through the palate, subtle notes of Kawakawa and peppery horopito emerge. A slight hint of juniper on the finish with lingering cinnamon.

SERVING SUGGESTION: Enjoy with Fever-Tree Aromatic Tonic Water.

AWARDS: The Junipers, New Zealand Gin Awards – Gold (Matured), & Best in Class (Matured)

Huddled beneath the slopes of Mt. Taranaki in the town of Stratford which is full of Shakespearian references, like many of their gins, Fenton Street Distillery has grown out of its founders' restoration of their 1920s neo-classical building. They are one of the smallest commercial distilleries in New Zealand, making deliberately small 48 litre batches to achieve a genuinely handcrafted product.

A pseudo-barrel aged gin, The Pioneer was made to reflect the efforts of the early European settlers that came to New Zealand by taking the barrel to the gin rather than the gin to the barrel.

FENTON STREET GIN
Est. 2018
THE PIONEER
Genuinely handcrafted in very small batches
for Gin's sake! ...at the Fenton Street Distillery
NO ARTIFICIAL PRESERVATIVES
Drink for Flavour. Drink Less. Enjoy More.
Est. 2018
46% Alc.Vol.

Black Barn Syrah Barrel Aged Gin

44.2% ABV

DISTILLERY: imagination, Reikorangi

WEBSITE: imaginationgin.nz

BOTANICALS: Juniper, Coriander Seed, Cinnamon, Liquorice Root, Orris Root, Orange, Lime, Lemon & Manuka

---

AGING PROCESS: Aged in Toasted French Oak Barrel.

TASTING NOTES: Oaked vanilla with citrus peel and fragrant coriander on the nose. Savoury palate with toasted orange and cinnamon, finishing with floral juniper and a hint of peppercorn.

SERVING SUGGESTION: Enjoy neat or with Fever-Tree Soda Water.

AWARDS: SIP Awards – Silver 2020, IWSC – Bronze 2020, and NZ Spirits Awards – Bronze 2020

Sheltered in the lush foothills of the Reikorangi Valley on the Kapiti Coast, imagination is housed on the original site of the pioneering Tuatara Beer Brewery which they use to draw inspiration from. They produce small batch seasonal gins using a copper plate fractionating column still and pure rainwater captured on the property, and source many of their ingredients locally from family owned operations and backyard gardeners.

A barrel aged gin matured in lightly toasted French oak barrels, Black Barn Syrah Barrel Aged Gin is made with their highest quality triple distilled gin and has a dusky pink colour.

imagination
BB'20
BLACK BARN SYRAH
BARREL AGED
NEW ZEALAND GIN
ABV 44.2% | 700ml

Little Biddy Gin - Cask Age (Pinot Noir)
47% ABV

DISTILLERY: Reefton Distilling Co., Reefton
VISIT THEM: 10 Smith Street, Reefton
WEBSITE: reeftondistillingco.com

BOTANICALS: Horopito, Rimu, Tarata, Toatoa, Douglas Fir, Fresh Lemon Peel, Angelica, Cardamom, Cassia, Coriander Seed, Juniper, Liquorice Root & Orris Root

---

AGING PROCESS: Aged in European Oak Pinot Noir Cask for one month.

TASTING NOTES: Bold citrus, tarata and lemon freshness with an oaky, herbal fragrance on the nose. Juniper and citrus peel emerge on the palate with a peppery horopito and burst of cardamom on the finish.

SERVING SUGGESTION: Enjoy neat or with Fever-Tree Soda Water.

AWARDS: San Francisco World Spirits Competition – Silver 2020 & Design Award 2020 and NZ Spirits Awards – Silver 2020

Stationed deep in the Inangahua River Valley in the West Coast town of Reefton, Little Biddy is named in honour of the local legend Bridget 'Biddy' Goodwin, a pipe-smoking, gin-toting, 4-foot-tall gold prospector who lived in the 1800s. A modern distillery in an age-old town, they use large numbers of native botanicals from the surrounding rainforest to achieve a distinct West Coast flavour.

A barrel aged gin rested in European oak pinot noir casks for one month, Little Biddy Gin – Cask Aged (Pinot Noir) is their first limited release gin infused with vanilla, ginger, and dark fruit resulting in a golden amber colour.

GUIDE TO NEW ZEALAND GIN
— 2020 —
TASTERS' PICK

SMALL BATCH DISTILLED
LITTLE BIDDY
New Zealand Botanical Gin
VAPOUR INFUSED
CASK AGED
BOTTLE NO.
1/310
CASKED FOR
1 month
CASK TYPE
European Oak
CASK SEASONING
Pinot Noir
CASK SIZE
20ℓ×10
BOTTLED
1/10/19
DISTILLED BY
N. Secker
ABV
47%
700ml

CRAFT DISTILLERS OF MARTINBOROUGH

Reid + Reid Barrel Aged Gin

42% ABV

DISTILLERY: Reid + Reid Distillery, Martinborough
VISIT THEM: 145 Todds Road, Martinborough
WEBSITE: reidandreid.co.nz

BOTANICALS: Juniper, Coriander Seed, Angelica Root, Liquorice Root, Orris Root, Fennel Seed, Nutmeg, Cassia, Cardamom, Orange Peel, Kawakawa, Horopito & Manuka

---

AGING PROCESS: Aged 3 Months in Ex-Martinborough Pinot Noir French Oak Barrels.

TASTING NOTES: Aromatic orange zest with a subtle hint of nutmeg, vanilla and herbal fragrance on the nose. Dry palate with juniper, cardamom, and cinnamon, finishing with emerging orange and kawakawa.

SERVING SUGGESTION: Enjoy neat or with Fever-Tree Soda Water.

AWARDS: Do Not Compete

Based in the warm micro-climate of Martinborough in the Wairarapa that supports a thriving local agriculture and viticulture, Reid + Reid Distillery was founded in 2015 by two brothers with backgrounds in engineering and beverage production. They seek to challenge the perception of a 'classic' gin and promote New Zealand's unique native flora.

A barrel aged gin spending three months in ex-Martinborough pinot noir French oak barrels, Reid + Reid Barrel Aged Gin uses their Native Gin as its base and has a golden amber colour.

· EST 2015 ·
NEW ZEALAND
REID+REID
BARREL AGED GIN
DISTILLED WITH NATIVE NEW ZEALAND BOTANICALS

NAVY STRENGTH

CONTAINING NAVY STRENGTH GINS

Navy Strength Gin – Gins bottled at an alcohol strength of at least 57% ABV.

Broken Heart Navy Strength Gin
57% ABV

DISTILLERY: Broken Heart Spirits, Arrow Junction

VISIT THEM: 3 Whitechapel Road, Arrow Junction (by appointment)

WEBSITE: brokenheartspirits.com

BOTANICALS: Juniper, Coriander Seed, Lavender, Angelica Root & Others Not Disclosed

---

TASTING NOTES: Bold aromatic juniper with floral lavender and fresh lemon peel on the nose. Dry palate with bold aromatic juniper, subtle lemon and floral spice emerges through the finish.

SERVING SUGGESTION: Enjoy with Fever-Tree Aromatic Tonic Water and a slice of lemon.

Nestled in the foothills of the Southern Alps near picturesque Arrowtown, Broken Heart Spirits was born from the memory of a beloved life lost. They endeavour to create gin that captures the glory days of a friendship between two Germans that met in the South Island and bonded over their mutual appreciation for creating fine spirits before one of them tragically passed away.

A navy gin with a potency of 57%, Broken Heart Navy Gin is based on their original Gin but with a stronger botanical flavour and impact.

GUIDE TO NEW ZEALAND GIN
— 2020 —
TASTERS'
PICK

Dancing Sands Wasabi Strength Gin
58% ABV

DISTILLERY: Dancing Sands Distillery, Takaka
VISIT THEM: 46A Commercial Street, Takaka
WEBSITE: dancingsands.com

BOTANICALS: Juniper, Coriander Seed, Angelica Root, Manuka, Cardamom, Peppercorn, Almond, Liquorice Root, Wasabi Root, Kelp, Horopito & Orange

---

TASTING NOTES: Light juniper with orange, liquorice, and earthy pepper on the nose. Bold juniper on the palate that carries subtle wasabi and peppery spice through to the finish.

SERVING SUGGESTION: Enjoy with Fever-Tree Aromatic Tonic Water and a slice of orange.

AWARDS: San Francisco World Spirit Awards – Gold Medal 2019, IWSC – Silver (91 pts) 2019, and NZ Spirit Awards – Double Gold 2020

Bundled away in the small town of Takaka in the Tasman region's beautiful Golden Bay area, Dancing Sands Distillery sources their water from the aquifer that feeds the nearby Te Waikoropupū Springs, often regarded as the clearest spring water in the world. They make all of their gins in small 150 litre batches to allow for maximum control over quality without any automation, instead using taste, temperature, and touch to achieve their results.

A navy strength gin with a potency of 58%, Dancing Sands Wasabi Strength Gin is made using two unique botanicals, kelp and locally grown wasabi root.

DANCING SANDS
••• WASABI GIN •••
58% ABV
700ML
HANDCRAFTED & MADE IN
NEW ZEALAND

Navy Strength Island Gin
57% ABV

DISTILLERY: Island Gin Distillery, Great Barrier Island
WEBSITE: islandgin.com

BOTANICALS: Juniper, Manuka & Bush Honey, Coriander Seed, Lemon Myrtle & Others Not Disclosed

---

TASTING NOTES: Bold aromatic juniper with fragrant herbs and lemon zest on the nose. Dry juniper palate with balanced citrus into the finish with subtle cardamom spice.

SERVING SUGGESTION: Enjoy with Fever-Tree Mediterranean Tonic Water and a slice of lemon.

AWARDS: NZ Spirits Award — Silver 2020

Secreted away on the remote but beautiful Great Barrier Island, Island Gin Distillery has a sustainable ethos towards producing their small batch gins. Their bottles are designed to reflect a Kina shell and are made with almost 50% reclaimed glass, meaning that just like no two kina shells are alike neither are their bottles. All of their gins are distilled in small batches using a copper still before heading to their solar-powered bottling line.

A navy strength gin with a potency of 57%, Navy Strength Island Gin wis nicknamed "Shark Alley" because it is "not for the faint of heart"!

57.0% ABV
700ml
Navy Strength
Small batch
distilled with
Great Barrier
Island Manuka
ISLAND
GIN
GT
BARRIER
ISL
N Z

Lighthouse Gin Hawthorn Edition
57% ABV

DISTILLERY: Lighthouse Distillery, Martinborough
WEBSITE: lighthousegin.co.nz

BOTANICALS: Juniper, Coriander Seed, Yen Ben Lemon Zest, Navel Orange Zest, Cinnamon, Almond, Cassia Bark, Orris Root & Liquorice Root

---

TASTING NOTES: Aromatic juniper with savoury toasted almond and orange zest on the nose. Bold juniper with zesty orange and earthy root notes on the palate, dry bold finish with lingering spice.

SERVING SUGGESTION: Enjoy with Fever-Tree Aromatic Tonic Water and a slice of orange.

Located in the warm micro-climate of Martinborough in the Wairarapa that supports a thriving local agriculture and viticulture, Lighthouse Distillery is one of New Zealand's oldest craft gins. Taking inspiration from the region's iconic Cape Palliser Lighthouse and its association with craftsmanship, they only use the purest water filtered from high in the nearby Remutaka Ranges in their twice distilled gins.

A navy gin with a potency of 57%, Lighthouse Gin Hawthorn Edition is inspired by a Wellington institution the Hawthorn Lounge an intimate speakeasy with a focus on cocktails.

RACHEL HALL
DISTILLER
NEW ZEALAND
LIMITED EDITION
EST.05
HAND CRAFTED
LIGHTHOUSE
BATCH DISTILLED
GIN
HAWTHORN EDITION
DISTILLED AND BOTTLED
IN NEW ZEALAND
57% ALC VOL. 700 ML
DOUBLE DISTILLED
BATCH

Scapegrace Gold

57% ABV

DISTILLERY: Scapegrace Distilling Co., Christchurch

WEBSITE: scapegracedistillery.com

BOTANICALS: Lemon Peel, Orange Peel, Corander Seed, Cardamom, Nutmeg, Juniper, Angelica Root, Liquorice Root, Orris Root, Clove, Cinnamon, Cassia Bark & Tangerine

---

TASTING NOTES: Bold aromatic juniper with heavy citrus and spiced nutty characters on the nose. Savoury palate of cardamom and nutmeg with notes of orange peel followed by developing citrus and a bold navy-strength style finish.

SERVING SUGGESTION: : Enjoy with Fever-Tree Premium Indian Tonic Water and a slice of orange.

AWARDS: IWSC — Trophy Winner, Voted World's Best London Dry 2018, and San Francisco World Spirits Competition — Gold 2017 & 2016, Double Gold 2018

Tucked away in the 'Garden City' of Christchurch, Scapegrace Distilling Co. makes their gin using glacial water that takes 80 years to filter through the rock of the Southern Alps before being released into an aquifer. They use a restored 19th century hand-beaten copper pot still to create their gins in the same way it was done back then. This is reflected in their bottles which are a modern take on the genever (Dutch gin) bottles from 200 years ago.

A navy gin with a potency of 57%, Scapegrace Gold is a London Dry Gin with three layers of citrus, orange, lemon, and tangerine.

BATCH N°
001
01
500
DISTILLED IN
NEW ZEALAND
N
SMALL PREMIUM BATCH
SCAPEGRACE
W E
DRY GIN
NEW ZEALAND
GOLD
HANDCRAFTED
ARTISAN GIN
57% ABV
700ml

IF 3/4 OF YOUR DRINK IS THE MIXER, MIX WITH THE BEST
FEVER-TREE
TONIC WATER
FEVER-TREE
PREMIUM INDIAN
TONIC WATER
200ml
FEVER-TREE
MEDITERRANEAN
TONIC WATER
200ml
FEVER-TREE

A SHORT HISTORY OF TONIC

NO CARBONATION, NO TONIC. NO TONIC, NO FEVER-TREE!
Does not bear thinking about. We have gin, we have ice and now we have carbonation. But what about tonic?

To find the answer to that question you only have to look at the name itself. You see, unlike gin, tonic really does have medicinal qualities to it. Or at least, quinine which is found in the bark of the Cinchona Tree from which Tonic is made does (and just as well too). In the 1600's, with the world plagued by malaria carrying mosquitos, a Jesuit monk called Agostino (Jesuits were considered the geniuses of the time) discovered that native Indians who would chew the Cinchona bark when they had fever would see their fever subside.

So, he wondered whether it could do the same with Malaria – and hey presto! The medicine was sent all over Europe and for the first time ever there was a way to prevent the epidemic spreading.

In the 1800s, we saw the first 'Indian Tonic Waters' created as the British soldiers stationed in India mixed their daily ration of quinine with 'a spoonful of sugar to help the medicine go down' along with some local spices and citrus. That little Cinchona bark pretty much changed the world. These enterprising soldiers and their counter parts in the Royal Navy couldn't resist mixing this medicinal mixture with their ration of gin. The humble G&T. This little concoction revolutionised the way people took their daily medicine and also when they took it. With the mosquitos choosing to come out as the sun went down, all over Europe people would raise a glass at sunset and enjoy a gin and tonic as a pleasantly social ritual.

In London, gin's reputation was on the rise. So much was gin's transformation that it inspired one London-based gentleman, an Erasmus Bond, to come up with the simple, yet wonderful idea of a pre-made tonic. In doing so, the social status of the drink had now been well and truly elevated.

DID YOU KNOW?
Under a UV light, the quinine in tonic water makes the water fluoresce a brilliant bright blue.

SIR WINSTON CHURCHILL SAID...
"Gin and tonic has saved more Englishmen's lives, and minds, than all the doctors in the Empire!"

HOW TO CREATE THE PERFECT GIN & TONIC

It all began in 2003 with a meeting of minds and one simple premise: if three quarters of your G&T is the tonic, wouldn't you want it to be the best?

REIGNITING A LONG-FORGOTTEN AND NEGLECTED SECTOR OF THE DRINKS INDUSTRY

Our co-founders Charles and Tim, working in different parts of the drinks business, had both spotted that premium spirits were growing quickly, fuelled by consumers' increasing awareness of the provenance of what they ate and drank.

However, this growing interest in premium food and drink had seemed to neglect mixers, a crucial element of the drinks industry that remained flat. It struck them both as extraordinary that people were paying a good deal of money for a high-quality spirit, yet had no choice but drown it with a poor-quality mixer

CHARLES AND TIM SET OUT TO PUT QUALITY BACK INTO MIXERS

From the very beginning, Charles and Tim approached their business in a different way – there would be no compromise at Fever-Tree. Flavour and quality were of the utmost importance. This mindset led them on an 18-month adventure from the archives of the British Library to facing the wrong end of a Kalashnikov in the Democratic Republic of Congo and concluded with the launch of our Premium Indian Tonic Water in 2005, with the belief we still operate by today…

PIONEERING TO PRODUCE AN UNRIVALLED DRINKING EXPERIENCE AT EVERY OCCASION

Since we put the lid on our first bottle of our Premium Indian Tonic Water, we haven't wavered in our single-minded mission to bring quality, flavour and choice back to mixers. Innovation remains at the heart of Fever-Tree and we've developed an award winning range of tonic waters that perfectly complement the varied flavour categories of gin. We've found three incredibly diverse varieties of ginger that, together, create a remarkably deep, fresh and true taste, which we've used to make a selection of ginger ales and ginger beer. We have lemonades using the finest,

naturally sourced ingredients and have recently launched our Soda Collection – A brand-new range of three mouth-watering flavoured sodas, including Lime & Yuzu, Italian Blood Orange and Pink Grapefruit. Our story is about going to the ends of the earth in pursuit of the best and, the most exciting thing is, we've only just scratched the surface.

OUR MIXERS

We start with the idea that, if ¾ of your drink is the mixer, then you should use the best. We work with only the best naturally sourced ingredients from around the world and no artificial flavourings or sweeteners to create mixers that do justice to the world's finest spirits

PAIR YOUR FAVOURITE PREMIUM GINS WITH FEVER-TREE MIXERS

Gin is an often overlooked spirit, despite its incredibly rich diversity. Bursts of juicy citrus, deliciously savoury herb notes and crisp, floral flavours are just some of the immense range of characteristics this one spirit can contain. Fever-Tree has been on a relentless pioneering pursuit to create a selection of award-winning tonic waters, each one individually crafted to complement the diverse flavour profiles of gin. While made with gins in mind, our tonics pair equally as well.

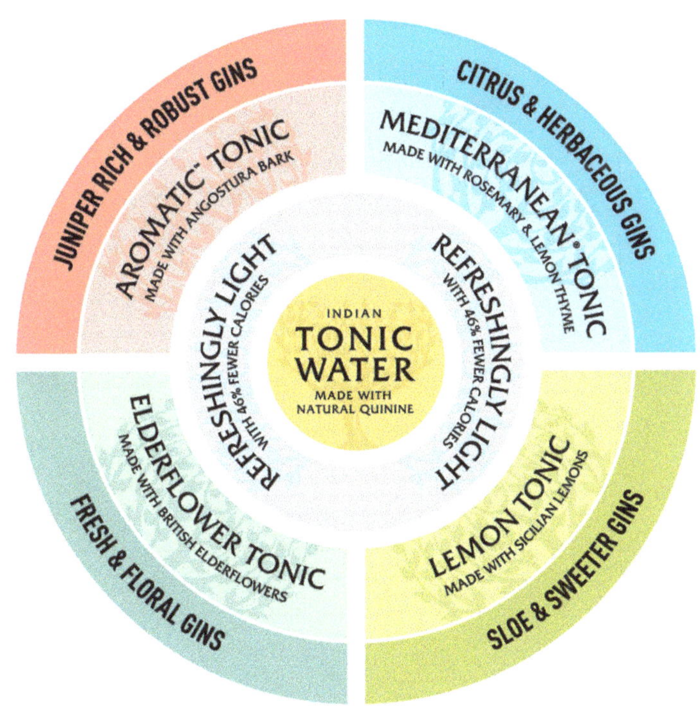

TONICS

PREMIUM INDIAN TONIC WATER

By blending luscious botanical oils with spring water and quinine of the highest quality from the 'fever trees' from the eastern hill ranges of the Democratic Republic of Congo, we have created a delicious, award-winning tonic water. Designed to enhance the very best gins, vodkas and fortified wines, like vermouth, fino sherry and white port.

REFRESHINGLY LIGHT INDIAN TONIC WATER

We use naturally occurring fruit sugars to develop our lighter tonic water. The blending of subtle botanical flavours with spring water and highest-quality quinine gives it the distinctively clean, crisp character of Indian Tonic Water, but with 46% fewer calories.

MEDITERRANEAN TONIC WATER

By blending the essential oils from the flowers, fruits and herbs that we have gathered from around the Mediterranean shores with highest-quality quinine from the 'fever trees' of the Democratic Republic of the Congo, we have created a delicate, floral tonic water.

ELDERFLOWER TONIC WATER

By blending the essential oils from handpicked English elderflowers with quinine of the highest quality from the 'fever trees' of the Democratic Republic of the Congo, we have created a delicious, floral variation of our Indian tonic water.

AROMATIC TONIC WATER

By blending the gentle bitterness of South American angostura bark with aromatic botanicals, such as cardamom, pimento berry and ginger, we've created a delicious, unique tonic water that can be enjoyed with gin to make a Pink G&T or as a sophisticated soft drink on its own.

LEMON TONIC WATER

By blending the finest Sicilian lemons with spring water and quinine of the highest quality from the fever trees of the Democratic Republic of the Congo, we have created a delicious lemon tonic water with an authentic refreshing taste and aroma.

REFRESHINGLY LIGHT
CUCUMBER TONIC WATER

Offering a delicate and fresh flavour, the light, crisp notes of cucumber essence are perfectly balanced with the gentle bitterness of our signature quinine from the fever trees of Eastern Congo. Blended with fruit sugar for 32% fewer calories than Fever-Tree Indian Tonic Water. The result is a tonic with an authentic and refreshing taste and aroma.

REFRESHINGLY LIGHT
CLEMENTINE TONIC WATER

Fresh Clementine's and Sri Lankan Cinnamon blends beautifully with the highest quality quinine from the Democratic Republic of Congo creating a delicately balanced tonic, complimenting premium sweetly spiced & sloe gins impeccably.

GINGERS

GINGER BEER

By brewing a blend of three gingers from Nigeria, Cochin and the Ivory Coast, we have created an award-winning ginger beer that has been highly acclaimed by gastronomes and critics alike. Not too sweet on the palate and with a deep, long-lasting ginger character. Perfect in a Dark & Stormy, Moscow Mule or simply as a soft drink on its own.

GINGER ALE

By using a unique blend of three of the world's finest naturally sourced gingers, subtle botanical flavours and spring water, we have created a delicious Ginger Ale with an authentic and refreshing taste and aroma. Perfectly balanced to enhance the flavour notes of the finest whiskies, bourbons and rums.

SMOKY GINGER ALE

We have combined our signature blend of three varieties of ginger with smoked applewood and subtle citrus to create a unique mixer that has been designed to enhance the finest whiskies and bourbons

SPICED ORANGE GINGER ALE

A unique blend of our signature gingers, combined with sweet clementine's and spicy cinnamon. The combination of ginger, citrus and spice has been crafted to complement the rich, full-bodied flavours found in the finest dark spirits, in particular cognacs & rums.

SODAS

PREMIUM SODA WATER

By using soft spring water, bicarbonate of soda and a high level of carbonation, we've have created a delicious soda water with a delicate aroma. Perfect for bringing out the best flavours of the finest whiskies.

PINK GRAPEFRUIT SODA

Made with real juice from handpicked pink Florida grapefruits. An impressive upfront burst of fresh grapefruit carefully balanced with soft pink grapefruit floral notes. The perfect levels of carbonation and real juice content provide a rounded base which complements the best premium tequilas and vodkas for a refreshing, light spritz.

ITALIAN BLOOD ORANGE SODA

Juicy blood oranges from Sicily meet an iconic herbal blend to create our Italian Blood Orange Soda. This complex and sophisticated mixer pairs perfectly with premium vodka and Italian liqueurs.

LIME AND YUZU SODA

Our Lime and Yuzu Soda is made with Tahiti lime from Mexico's fertile groves in addition to pressed oil extract from the wonderfully floral Japanese yuzu to create a low-calorie soda that's perfect for mixing with premium vodka or tequila for a mouth-wateringly zesty summer spritz.

GUIDE TO NEW ZEALAND GIN